HOLIDAY
SLOW COOKER

Delicious Recipes for a Year of Hassle-Free Celebrations

Jonnie Downing

Ulysses Press

To my precious daughter, Elizabeth

Published by:
Ulysses Press
P.O. Box 3440
Berkeley, CA 94703
www.ulyssespress.com

ISBN: 978-1-61243-102-4
Library of Congress Catalog Number 2012940435

Printed in the United States by Bang Printing

10 9 8 7 6 5 4 3 2 1

Acquisitions editor: Kelly Reed
Managing editor: Claire Chun
Editor: Phyllis Elving
Proofreader: Lauren Harrison
Design and layout: what!design @ whatweb.com
Cover photographs: © JudiSwinksPhotography.com
Interior photographs: see page 105
Food stylist for featured recipes: Anna Hartman-Kenzler

Distributed by Publishers Group West

TABLE OF CONTENTS

INTRODUCTION 1

RINGING IN THE YEAR

New Year's Day
Bacon-Wrapped Cocktail Weenies 4
Party Mix 5
Meatballs in Tangy Sauce 7
Piquant Black-Eyed Peas 8
Pork Loin with Wine Sauce 9
Liberty Brownie Squares 10

Presidents' Day
Thomas Jefferson's Chicken Fricassee 11
Lyndon Johnson's Chili 12
Jackie Kennedy's Beef Stroganoff 13
Ronald Reagan's Hamburger Soup 14

Mardi Gras
Hoppin' John 15
Easy, Delicious Gumbo 16
Mock Turtle Soup 17

Valentine's Day
Cheese Fondue 18
Lobster Bisque 19
Beef Bourguignon 20
Rocky Road Pudding Cake 21
Milk Chocolate Fondue 22
Baileys Hot Chocolate 24

St. Patrick's Day
Slow-Baked Potatoes 25
Party Sausages and Peppers 26
Traditional Guinness Stew 27
Classic Corned Beef and Cabbage 29

Easter
Potatoes au Gratin 30
Egg Casserole 31
Split Pea Soup with Ham 32
Leg of Lamb 33
Honey-Glazed Ham 34
Almond Cheesecake 36

FUN IN THE SUN

Cinco de Mayo
Tortilla Soup 38
Pinto Beans 39
Carnitas 41
Chicken Enchiladas 42
Mexican Braised Beef 43
Caramel Flan 44

Mother's Day Brunch
French Toast Casserole 45
Breakfast Quiche 46
Loaded Potatoes 47

Father's Day Sides
Beer Baked Beans 48
Creamy Macaroni and Cheese 49
Cheesy Bacony Potatoes 50

Fourth of July
Crab Dip 51
Bourbon Bacon Baked Beans 52
Buffalo Chicken Wings 53
Pulled Pork 54
BBQ Beef 56
Baked Apple Crisp 57

Bastille Day
Squash Bisque 58
Ratatouille 59
Boeuf en Daube 60
Chicken Provençal Stew 61
Coq Au Vin 62

FALL CELEBRATIONS

Oktoberfest
Kielbasa and Kraut 64
Oktoberfest Short Ribs 65

Halloween
Halloween Pumpkin Soup 66
Perfect Wild Rice Pilaf 67
Autumn Pork Stew 69
S'more Fondue 70

Thanksgiving

Silky Smooth Sweet Potato Purée...71
Buttery Mashed Potatoes 72
Classic Green Bean Casserole 74
Sweet Potato Casserole 75
Heavenly Squash and Apples 76
Cornbread Dressing 77
Easy Turkey Breast 78
Savory Stuffed Cornish Game Hens 79
Easy Tender Turkey Legs 81
Turkey Soup with Dumplings 82
Sweet and Easy Cranberry Sauce..83
Pumpkin Butter 84
Pumpkin Custard 85

HAPPY HOLIDAYS

Christmas

Creamy Scalloped Potatoes 88
Brussels Sprouts with Spicy Brown Mustard 89
Candied Sweet Potatoes 90
Hearty Root Vegetable Stew 91
Christmas Lamb Roast..92
Maple Brown Sugar Ham 94
Succulent Beef Tenderloin 95
Sugar-Baked Apples 96
Cinnamon Bread Pudding...97
Hot Apple Cider 98

Hanukkah

Maple Carrots 99
Slow Cooker Kugel 100
Old-Fashioned Beef Brisket 101
Braised Lamb Shanks..102
Chunky Applesauce 103
Challah Pudding...104

Conversions..105
Photo Credits..105
About the Author 106
Acknowledgments...106

INTRODUCTION

Slow cooking is a great way to cook a fabulous meal. You simply throw the right things in the slow cooker, set the temperature, and walk away. What comes out is almost always good.

Slow cookers have been around since the 1970s, and they have been instrumental in taking the stress out of cooking—letting busy families enjoy time together rather than having the cook stuck in the kitchen. Holidays can be really hectic times, with family and friends visiting—making them joyous times as well. So the last thing you want is to spend all day in the kitchen. That's what your slow cooker is for. You can quickly prep classic holiday dishes and let the slow cooker work its magic. The slow cooker stays in the kitchen all day so that you don't have to.

This book contains many traditional holiday meals as well as new dishes to liven up your celebrations. These are fun and easy recipes, requiring minimal work and far less cleanup time than the average holiday dinner.

Using a Slow Cooker

Odds are you already own a slow cooker. Maybe it was your first college gift, your first apartment gift, or maybe you got two or three when you got married. Either way, you either use it all the time or you don't. That doesn't matter. It's never too late to start using your slow cooker. If you don't own a slow cooker, go get one!

If you're flying solo or just have one other diner, a 3- to 4-quart slow cooker is a great choice, but not for most recipes in this book. While you can modify these dishes to fit a smaller slow cooker, all these recipes are based on a 6-quart slow cooker, which will make enough to feed a large family or provide plenty of yummy leftovers for freezing or sharing. And that's what holidays are all about.

A few things you should know. One, you can't make *everything* in a slow cooker—but you can make *almost* everything. Be it a main course, side dish, dessert, or snack mix, the slow cooker is a versatile and powerful kitchen tool.

Whether to buy a round or oval slow cooker is a matter of preference. Round is more versatile and much easier to clean. However, for large pieces of meat, an oval slow cooker is best. If you're serious about slow cooking, I recommend you get one of each.

A slow cooker does just what it says—it cooks things slow. Most slow cookers have three settings: high, low, and warm. Most of the recipes in this book call for cooking on the low temperature, but pay close attention, because a few recipes call for cooking on high at first and then turning the temperature down to low. When in doubt, cook on low and cook for a long time.

A slow cooker is a very forgiving appliance, but you still need to follow a few simple rules. Don't put any sort of plastic or paper in your slow cooker. Follow recipes generally to know cooking times so things aren't over or underdone, but feel free to take some creative license. Have fun with it. That's what cooking is all about!

New Year's Day

Presidents' Day

Mardi Gras

Valentine's Day

St. Patrick's Day

Easter

RINGING IN THE YEAR

What better way to start out the year than with a New Year's Day celebration? In American homes, the day is spent watching big football games, so I've included delicious finger foods and heartier dishes sure to please even the rowdiest crowd of sports fans.

With the end of winter comes two of the most fun holidays to celebrate, Mardi Gras and St. Patrick's Day. When I think Mardi Gras, I think New Orleans, so I've included recipes for spicy, down-home cuisine. Of course, for St. Patty's on March 17, it's the traditional corned beef and cabbage.

During the Jewish observance of Passover in March/April, lamb is traditional for many families. That has carried over to the Christian celebration of Easter, with many people choosing lamb for Easter Sunday. Ham, though, is more common in the United States. Before refrigerators, pigs were slaughtered in the fall and the meat was cured to prevent spoiling. Curing takes time, so by Easter, the hams were ready.

Bacon-Wrapped Cocktail Weenies

Almost everyone loves cocktail weenies. And more than almost everyone loves bacon. Put the two together, and New Year's magic happens.

YIELD: 16 servings (about 3 weenies each)
PREP TIME: 10 minutes
COOK TIME: 5 hours

INGREDIENTS
2 pounds cocktail weenies
1 pound sliced bacon
½ cup spicy brown mustard, plus more to serve

Wrap each cocktail weenie in a whole slice of bacon and secure with a toothpick. Arrange bacon-wrapped sausages in a layer in the slow cooker and spread with a coating of spicy brown mustard. Keep layering and coating with mustard until everything is in the slow cooker.

Cover and cook on low for 5 hours, or until the bacon is completely cooked. Serve with mustard on the side.

New Year's Day

The "ball" that drops in New York's Times Square on New Year's Eve is made of Waterford crystal and weighs more than 1,000 pounds.

Luck—or what people consider lucky—really does vary from region to region:

- Eating noodles at midnight on New Year's Eve is a tradition at Buddhist temples.
- In the U.S. South, it's thought that eating greens such as cabbage, kale, collard greens, mustard greens, and spinach will bring money in the new year.
- In Poland, pickled herring signifies good luck for the coming year.

Party Mix

Party mix is always a hit. Instead of serving it in a single large bowl, offer it in individual bags or adorable popcorn boxes for a personal touch that also cuts down on germ-sharing.

YIELD: 24 servings
PREP TIME: 10 minutes
COOK TIME: About 2 hours

INGREDIENTS

3 cups Cheerios

3 cups Rice Chex

3 cups mini Melba toasts

3 cups Wheat Chex

3 cups pretzel sticks

1 (6-ounce) can mixed nuts

1 cup (2 sticks) salted butter, melted

3 tablespoons Worcestershire sauce

1½ teaspoons seasoned salt

¾ teaspoon onion powder

Mix together the first six ingredients (Cheerios through nuts) in the slow cooker. In a bowl, whisk together the melted butter, Worcestershire, seasoned salt, and onion powder. Pour the butter mixture over the ingredients in the slow cooker, mix everything together, and cook, uncovered, on high for 1½ hours. Reduce the power to low and cook for another 20 minutes. Spread the mixture on a rimmed cookie sheet to cool and dry.

Store in an airtight container until ready to serve.

Keeps for about a week.

Meatballs in Tangy Sauce

Making your own meatballs is well worth the effort if you have the time. But if you don't, skip the meatball-making part of this recipe and substitute fresh or frozen store-bought meatballs.

YIELD: 8 to 10 large meatballs
PREP TIME: 20 minutes
COOK TIME: 8 to 10 hours

MEATBALL INGREDIENTS
1 pound lean ground beef
½ cup milk
1 cup soft breadcrumbs
1 teaspoon salt
1 teaspoon black pepper

SAUCE INGREDIENTS
½ cup water
½ cup ketchup
2 tablespoons red wine vinegar
1½ teaspoons Worcestershire sauce
1 tablespoon granulated sugar
½ cup chopped green pepper
½ cup chopped onion

Spray the inside of the slow cooker with cooking spray. In a large bowl, mix together the ground beef, milk, breadcrumbs, salt, and pepper. Form into meatballs and place in the slow cooker.

In a separate bowl, whisk together the water, ketchup, vinegar, Worcestershire, and sugar. Stir in the chopped green pepper and onion. Pour the sauce over the meatballs in the slow cooker. Cover and cook on low for 8 to 10 hours.

Piquant Black-Eyed Peas

These black-eyed peas have some heat, but you can adjust that by reducing the amount of jalapeno and cayenne.

YIELD: 10 servings
PREP TIME: 10 minutes
COOK TIME: 8 hours

INGREDIENTS

6 cups water

1 chicken bouillon cube

1 pound dried black-eyed peas, sorted and rinsed

8 ounces diced ham (buy it pre-diced to save time)

4 slices bacon, cooked

1 medium onion, diced

2 garlic cloves, minced

1 red bell pepper, seeded and diced

1 jalapeno pepper, seeded and chopped very fine

½ teaspoon cayenne pepper

1½ teaspoons ground cumin

1 teaspoon black pepper

¼ teaspoon salt, or to taste

Pour the water into your slow cooker. Add the bouillon cube and stir until it dissolves.

In a separate bowl, stir together the black-eyed peas, ham, bacon, onion, garlic, red pepper, jalapeno, cayenne, cumin, pepper, and salt. Add the mixture to the slow cooker, cover, and cook on low for 8 hours, or until the beans are tender.

Pork Loin with Wine Sauce

For many of us, a pork loin is the way to go for New Year's Day dinner. It pairs well with steamed cabbage and Hoppin' John (page 15) and saves beautifully for sandwiches or tacos carnitas.

YIELD: 5 to 7 servings
PREP TIME: 5 minutes
COOK TIME: 4 hours

INGREDIENTS

1 (2-pound) pork tenderloin
1 envelope dry onion soup mix
1 cup water
¾ cup dry red wine
3 tablespoons soy sauce
3 tablespoons minced garlic
freshly ground black pepper

Place the pork tenderloin, soup packet, water, wine, and soy sauce in the slow cooker (in that order). Roll the tenderloin around to coat it in the other ingredients. Spread the minced garlic over the top and add a few grinds of pepper.

Cover and cook on low for 4 hours, or until the internal temperature of the pork reaches between 155°F and 160°F. Remove and let sit, covered, for 15 minutes before slicing.

Liberty Brownie Squares

Brownies are a hit at any cookout. Just dust them with confectioners' sugar to serve — you'll be the most important person at the party. It's quicker to cook brownies in the oven, but more hassle-free to cook them in the slow cooker. The brownies will be soft and gooey, with crispy edges and wonderful flavor.

YIELD: 10 to 12 servings
PREP TIME: 20 minutes
COOK TIME: About 3 hours

INGREDIENTS

8 ounces bittersweet chocolate, chopped

1 ounce milk chocolate, chopped

½ cup (1 stick) unsalted butter, cut into tablespoon-size pieces

1 cup granulated sugar

3 eggs, beaten

1¼ cups all-purpose flour

¼ cup unsweetened cocoa powder

¾ teaspoon baking powder

½ teaspoon salt

1 cup semisweet chocolate chips

confectioners' sugar, for dusting (optional)

Spray the inside of the slow cooker with cooking spray. Line the bottom of the cooker with parchment paper (not waxed paper) and spray the top of the paper with cooking spray.

In the microwave oven, melt the bittersweet and milk chocolates together with the butter in a microwave-safe bowl, at medium-power, checking frequently to make sure the mixture doesn't burn. Alternatively, you can melt the chocolate and butter on the stovetop in a double boiler. Stir every 30 seconds until the chocolate is fully melted. Add the sugar and mix well. Add the beaten eggs and blend vigorously with a spoon, until the mixture is smooth.

Add the flour, cocoa powder, baking powder, salt, and chocolate chips, stirring until just blended (don't overmix). Pour the batter into the slow cooker and flatten the top. Cover and cook on low for 2 hours and 15 minutes. Remove the cover and continue cooking until done, about 20 minutes longer.

Using a knife to loosen the brownie, transfer it in one big piece, along with the parchment paper, to a cooling rack. Cool for 20 minutes, dust with confectioners' sugar if desired, and cut into serving-size pieces.

Thomas Jefferson's Chicken Fricassee

Thomas Jefferson was quite an avid farmer. At his Monticello plantation home in Virginia, he grew vegetables and actually wrote a cookbook. This is a modified version of Jefferson's own recipe — made slow cooker–friendly!

YIELD: 10 to 12 servings
PREP TIME: 20 minutes
COOK TIME: 6 hours

INGREDIENTS

6 boneless, skinless chicken breast halves

2 tablespoons unsalted butter

2 garlic cloves, chopped

3 tablespoons unbleached all-purpose flour

2 cups chicken broth (homemade is best, if you have it)

¼ teaspoon ground nutmeg

2 teaspoons chopped fresh thyme

1 teaspoon dried tarragon

4 carrots, peeled and chopped

2 medium yellow onions, cut into large pieces

8 white fingerling potatoes, scrubbed

2 leeks, white part only, chopped

1 bay leaf

1 cup fresh or frozen peas

½ cup cream

salt and pepper

Rinse the chicken breasts and pat dry with paper towels; cover and set aside. Melt the butter in a saucepan over medium heat and sauté the garlic in it briefly, until soft but not browned. Remove the garlic and add the flour, a bit at a time, stirring until you have a smooth roux. Slowly pour in the chicken broth, stirring constantly. Add the nutmeg, thyme, and tarragon. Keep stirring until the mixture thickens and begins to bubble.

In the slow cooker, layer the carrots, onions, and potatoes, then the chicken breasts, and finally the leeks. Pour the thickened sauce over the meat and vegetables and toss in the bay leaf.

Cover and cook on low for 6 hours, adding the peas and cream at 5 hours and 40 minutes and turning the temperature to high at that time. Season to taste with salt and pepper. Remove the bay leaf and ladle the stew into bowls to serve along with hunks of crusty bread.

Presidents' Day

Presidents' Day started out as Washington's Birthday (February 22) and was declared a federal holiday in 1885. Some states also celebrated Lincoln's birthday (February 12). Since 1971, Presidents' Day has been observed on the third Monday of February.

Ulysses S. Grant once got a ticket for exceeding the speed limit—on a horse.

Lyndon Johnson's Chili

This recipe is a modification of the Pedernales River Chili that Mrs. Lyndon Johnson prepared for her husband. Named for the hill country region where the Johnsons had their ranch, this Texas-style chili was reportedly a big favorite of the president's. Lady Bird made her chili in a Dutch oven, but it's super easy to fix in the slow cooker.

YIELD: 10 to 12 servings
PREP TIME: 15 minutes
COOK TIME: 5 to 6 hours

INGREDIENTS

4 pounds extra-lean ground beef

1 large yellow onion, finely chopped

2 garlic cloves, chopped

1½ (14-ounce) cans whole tomatoes, with liquid

2 cups hot water

6 splashes hot sauce (I use homemade, but Tabasco or Texas Pete's works just fine)

1 teaspoon dried oregano

2 tablespoons high-quality chili powder

½ teaspoon black pepper

salt

Note: Lady Bird's recipe also calls for "comino seed," but I don't happen to care for cumin seeds. If you do, add 1 teaspoon of them.

Brown the meat in a large skillet over medium heat, stirring to break it up; drain. Transfer into the slow cooker and layer on the vegetables, water, and seasonings. Cover and cook on low for 5 to 6 hours, stirring occasionally. Add salt to taste, as needed.

Jackie Kennedy's Beef Stroganoff

Was there anything this amazing woman wasn't good at? Try the first lady's delicious beef stroganoff recipe and judge for yourself.While this version is modified for the slow cooker, you'll still need to do some prep work. It's worth it.

YIELD: 6 to 8 servings
PREP TIME: 15 minutes
COOK TIME: 10 hours

INGREDIENTS

2 pounds top sirloin, trimmed of fat and cut into 2-inch strips

¼ teaspoon salt

¼ teaspoon pepper

¼ cup grated yellow onion

1½ cups sliced button mushrooms

2 cups beef broth

1 tablespoon tomato paste

1 teaspoon onion powder

egg noodles, for serving

½ cup sour cream

Spray the inside of the slow cooker with cooking spray. Season the beef strips with the salt and pepper and place in the slow cooker. Add the onion, mushrooms, broth, tomato paste, and onion powder. Cover and cook on low for 10 hours, until the beef is tender.

Shortly before serving time, cook the noodles according to the package directions. While they are cooking, mix the sour cream into the meat mixture in the slow cooker. Taste and adjust seasoning with salt and pepper, as needed. Serve the hot stroganoff over the noodles.

Ronald Reagan's Hamburger Soup

The Gipper's favorite hamburger soup is easy to prepare and satisfyingly tasty. I've made a few modifications for this slow cooker version. For instance, I serve it with elbow pasta rather than the hominy that the former president liked.

YIELD: 4 to 6 servings
PREP TIME: 15 minutes
COOK TIME: 8 hours

INGREDIENTS

2 pounds ground sirloin

2 cups diced yellow onion

2 garlic cloves, chopped

1½ cups peeled and sliced carrots

1 cup diced yellow or orange bell pepper (the original recipe calls for green, but I prefer yellow or orange)

1 pound fresh tomatoes, chopped

2 cups sliced celery

water

¼ teaspoon salt

¼ teaspoon pepper

elbow macaroni, for serving

Brown the meat in a skillet over medium heat, stirring to break it up; drain. Place the meat and all the vegetables (onion through celery) in the slow cooker. Season with the salt and pepper. Pour in water to about 1½ inches from the lip of the slow cooker.

Cover and cook on low for 8 hours, until the soup has thickened somewhat. Stir occasionally, and season with more salt and pepper to taste.

Cook the elbow macaroni according to the package directions, using the package guidelines for serving size. To serve, mix the soup with the pasta.

Hoppin' John

A fun take on black-eyed peas, this flavorful dish is a great treat when you make it yourself in the slow cooker rather than buying it in a can. Traditionally served on New Year's Day throughout the South (the peas represent coins and thus portend prosperity), Hoppin' John is equally at home on a Mardi Gras menu.

YIELD: 3 to 4 servings
PREP TIME: 10 minutes
COOK TIME: 8 hours

INGREDIENTS

4 slices center-cut bacon, diced

1 small onion, diced

1 cup dried black-eyed peas, sorted and rinsed

½ teaspoon crushed red pepper

1 teaspoon salt, plus more as needed

4 cups water

1 (14.5-ounce) can diced tomatoes, drained

2 teaspoons diced pickled jalapenos

Cook the bacon in a skillet over medium-high heat until almost crisp. Add the diced onion and cook until soft. Transfer the bacon, onions, and all the drippings into the slow cooker. Add the black-eyed peas, crushed red pepper, and 1 teaspoon salt. Top with the water.

Cover and cook on low for 4 hours, or until the black-eyed peas are tender. Then stir in the tomatoes, jalapenos, and a bit more salt, if needed. Cook until reduced, until the added liquid is mostly absorbed.

Mardi Gras

Mardi Gras dates back to medieval times, but in New Orleans it commemorates the 1699 landing of French explorers Pierre Le Moyne d'Iberville and Jean Baptiste Le Moyne de Bienville just south of the present-day city.

Mardi Gras ends on Ash Wednesday, when the time of excess is over and Lent begins.

New Orleans's oldest parade group, or krewe, the Mystick Krewe of Comus, was founded in 1856.

Easy, Delicious Gumbo

You'll feel like a real N'Awlins native when you dish this up for your guests.

YIELDS: 6 to 8 servings
PREP TIME: 30 minutes
COOK TIME: 8 hours

INGREDIENTS

1 tablespoon olive oil

2 teaspoons minced garlic

1 medium yellow onion, diced

3 medium carrots, peeled and sliced

1 cup fresh corn kernels

½ green pepper, seeded and diced

½ red pepper, seeded and diced

1 pound boneless, skinless chicken breasts, cut into bite-sized chunks

3 cups chicken stock, divided (homemade is best, if you have it)

2 tablespoons Worcestershire sauce

1 teaspoon Cajun seasoning blend

1 teaspoon chili powder

¼ teaspoon salt

¼ teaspoon pepper

2 cups diced tomatoes

2 tablespoons olive oil

1 pound andouille sausages, cut into 1-inch pieces

2 tablespoons all-purpose flour

8 ounces raw shrimp, peeled and deveined

6 cups cooked rice, for serving

Warm the olive oil in a large skillet over medium heat, and sauté the garlic, onion, carrots, corn, and peppers. Place the cooked vegetables in the slow cooker along with the chicken, 2 cups of the stock, the Worcestershire, Cajun seasoning, chili powder, salt, and pepper.

Brown the andouille pieces in the same skillet you used for the vegetables, turning to brown all sides. Reduce the heat to low and cover to cook through, about 15 minutes. Add the andouille to the slow cooker, reserving 2 tablespoons of the sausage drippings in the skillet. Discard the remaining drippings.

Whisk the flour into the reserved sausage drippings in the skillet. Add the remaining 1 cup stock and stir until smooth and thickened. Pour over the ingredients in the slow cooker, cover, and cook on low for 8 hours.

Fifteen minutes before the end of the cooking time, stir in the shrimp. Cook, covered, until the shrimp turns pink. Serve the gumbo over cooked rice.

Mock Turtle Soup

Originally created to imitate the expensive green turtle soup favored by the elite of Victorian England, mock turtle soup makes a satisfying Mardi Gras meal in this Cajun interpretation.

YIELDS: 6 to 8 servings
PREP TIME: 20 minutes
COOK TIME: 5 to 6 hours

INGREDIENTS

½ cup canola oil

½ pound boneless chuck roast, chopped into bite-size pieces

½ pound pork butt, chopped into bite-size pieces

½ pound chicken, boneless, skinless white and dark meat, chopped into bite-size pieces

¾ cup all-purpose flour

1 cup chopped yellow onion

½ cup finely chopped green onions, white and green parts

2 tablespoons chopped celery

½ cup finely chopped fresh parsley

10 cups beef stock, beef broth, or water

½ cup tomato sauce

2 hard-cooked eggs, chopped

2 tablespoons hot sauce

salt

Heat the oil in a large skillet over medium heat. Brown all the meat together in the oil, making sure the pieces are browned on all sides. Transfer the meat to the slow cooker. In the skillet, whisk the flour into the drippings in the pan to make a roux. It will be dark — that's okay.

Toss the yellow and green onions, celery, and parsley into the skillet and cook until the onions are translucent. Add 1 cup of the beef stock or water and stir to form a paste. Add the tomato sauce and mix thoroughly. Transfer to the slow cooker along with the meat, eggs, hot sauce, and the remaining stock or water. Season to taste with salt. Cover and cook on low for 5 to 6 hours.

MARDI GRAS

Cheese Fondue

YIELD: 12 to 15 servings
PREP TIME: 10 minutes
COOK TIME: 2 hours

INGREDIENTS

8 ounces Gruyère cheese, shredded

8 ounces fontina cheese, shredded

2 tablespoons all-purpose flour

½ teaspoon dry mustard

¾ cup Pinot Grigio wine

French bread and bite-size raw vegetables, to serve

In a bowl, mix together the cheeses, flour, and dry mustard. Pour the wine into the slow cooker and heat on low for about 15 minutes. When it is warm, stir in half the cheese mixture. When the cheese is nicely melted, stir in the rest of the cheese and cover. Let all the cheese melt, at least 1 hour, and serve right away with chunks of French bread, bite-size raw vegetables, and anything else that will taste delicious covered in hot cheese.

Serve directly from the slow cooker with fondue forks or spears.

Valentine's Day

Everyone has an opinion about what's an aphrodisiac:

- Oysters are widely considered to be aphrodisiacs. (Since when does slimy = sensual?)
- In China, nutmeg is believed to be a powerful aphrodisiac for men.
- Figs are thrown at weddings in some southern European cultures. They are supposed to symbolize fertility.
- The scent of almonds is supposed to arouse the ladies.

Lobster Bisque

Oysters, traditionally considered an aphrodisiac, aren't so great in the slow cooker. A delicious lobster bisque, on the other hand, is. While it may not be thought of as a passion-igniter, this rich soup makes a lovely meal for a special romantic night. Something about decadence really brings out your romantic side, right?

YIELD: 10 servings
PREP TIME: 5 minutes
COOK TIME: 6 to 9 hours

INGREDIENTS

3 cups chicken broth

8 ounces bottled clam juice

1 (14.5-ounce) can stewed tomatoes, including liquid

8 ounces sliced button mushrooms

1 medium yellow onion, diced

1 large leek (white part only), diced

1 teaspoon dried parsley

2 teaspoons Old Bay Seasoning, plus some for sprinkling

1 teaspoon dried dill

uncooked meat of 2 fresh lobster tails, meat removed from tails and torn into chunks

1 cup heavy cream

Place everything except the lobster meat and cream in the slow cooker and stir together. Cover and cook on low for 6 to 8 hours, then use an immersion blender to blend the mixture to a smoother consistency. If you don't have an immersion blender, you can use a whisk, but the texture won't be as good.

Stir in the lobster meat, cover, and cook on high for another 30 to 45 minutes, until the lobster meat is opaque. Lift out the lobster meat and set aside. Using the immersion blender or whisk, stir in the heavy cream.

Ladle the bisque into bowls and top each serving with lobster meat and a dash of Old Bay.

Beef Bourguignon

This dish is a tad more labor-intensive than most of our slow cooker dishes, but cooking the beef in the slow cooker makes it much more tender than any other method.

YIELD: 8 servings
PREP TIME: 30 minutes
COOK TIME: 12 hours

VALENTINE'S DAY

INGREDIENTS

18 bacon slices, cut into 2-inch pieces

3 pounds boneless beef rump roast, trimmed of fat and cut into 1-inch cubes

½ cup all-purpose flour, divided

1 large carrot, peeled and sliced

1 medium yellow onion, sliced

1 teaspoon salt

½ teaspoon black pepper

1 (10.5-ounce) can condensed beef broth

1 tablespoon tomato paste

2 cups Burgundy wine (one you'd drink, not the cheapest you can find!)

1 pound button mushrooms, sliced ¼ inch thick

8 ounces white pearl onions, peeled

2 garlic cloves, minced

½ teaspoon dried thyme

1 bay leaf

Crisp the bacon pieces in a skillet over medium heat. Cutting the bacon into strips prior to frying it makes it cook up faster, so keep an eye on it. You'll end up with delicious little bites of crispy bacon — try not to eat them all before they go into the dish. Remove the bacon from the skillet and reserve.

Roll your beef cubes in enough flour to coat (save the rest) and drop them into the still-hot skillet with the bacon drippings. Brown the pieces very well on all sides and remove from the skillet. Set aside with the bacon.

Into the same skillet, brown the carrots and yellow onion. Transfer to the slow cooker and season liberally with the salt and pepper. Stir in the beef broth and the remaining flour, mixing well. Mix in the beef and the bacon and then add the tomato paste, wine, mushrooms, pearl onions, garlic, thyme, and bay leaf.

Cover and cook on low for 12 hours. Check once or twice while cooking to see if the seasoning needs adjusting; add salt and pepper to taste, as needed. Remove the bay leaf before serving.

Rocky Road Pudding Cake

For a sweet treat — and that adorable smudge of flour on your temple to show that you've really been working hard — try this sure-fire combination of chocolate, marshmallows, and nuts.

YIELD: 10 to 12 servings
PREP TIME: 10 minutes
COOK TIME: 5 hours

INGREDIENTS

1 (18.25-ounce) package German chocolate cake mix

1 (3.3-ounce) package chocolate instant pudding mix

3 large eggs, beaten

1 cup sour cream

⅓ cup unsalted butter, melted

1 teaspoon vanilla extract

3¼ cups milk, divided

1 (3.3-ounce) package chocolate cook-and-serve pudding mix

½ cup chopped pecans

1 cup semisweet chocolate chips

1½ cups plain miniature marshmallows

Using an electric mixer, beat together the cake mix, instant pudding mix, eggs, sour cream, butter, vanilla, and 1¼ cups of milk, mixing until smooth. Spray the slow cooker with cooking spray and pour in the batter.

In a copper or other nonreactive saucepan over medium-high heat, heat the remaining 2 cups of milk, stirring often. *Do not boil.* Heat just until a few bubbles appear.

Working quickly, sprinkle the cook-and-serve pudding mix over the batter in the slow cooker, then pour the hot milk over the pudding. Cover and cook on low for 3½ hours.

Shortly before the cake is finished, toast the pecans in a nonstick skillet over medium-low to medium heat. Stir to keep them from burning — you just want to heat them until they're a little toasted.

Uncover the slow cooker and scatter the pecans, chocolate chips, and marshmallows over the surface of the cake. Wait a few minutes for the marshmallows and chocolate chips to melt and then serve the warm pudding cake directly from the slow cooker.

Milk Chocolate Fondue

Nothing says Valentine's Day better than a vat of hot chocolate fondue, some yummy things to dip in it, and your sweetheart to share it with.

YIELD: 10 to 12 servings
PREP TIME: 10 minutes
COOK TIME: 45 minutes

VALENTINE'S DAY

INGREDIENTS

18 ounces semisweet chocolate, chopped

6 ounces milk chocolate, chopped

1 ounce unsweetened chocolate, chopped

¼ cup confectioners' sugar

1 (12-ounce) can evaporated milk

1 teaspoon vanilla extract

fresh fruit, chunks of pound cake, cookies, marshmallows, pretzels, and popcorn, to serve

Place the chocolates, sugar, and milk in the slow cooker. Cover and cook on low for 45 minutes. Stir, add the vanilla, and stir again.

Pass forks for dipping pieces of fruit, chunks of pound cake, cookies, and marshmallows into the chocolate fondue. Try to eat it all at once, as it doesn't keep well.

Baileys® Hot Chocolate

Hot chocolate can be a great thing on a cold February day. Hot chocolate with Baileys is even better. Just make the delicious hot chocolate in the slow cooker, then add a splash of Baileys Irish Cream to each cup. Yum! Of course, kids and other non-imbibers will enjoy the cocoa by itself.

YIELD: 16 servings
PREP TIME: 5 minutes
COOK TIME: About 1 hour

INGREDIENTS

1¼ cups unsweetened cocoa powder

1½ cups granulated sugar

1¼ teaspoons salt

¾ cup hot water

1 gallon whole milk

1 teaspoon vanilla extract

¼ teaspoon ground cinnamon

16 ounces Baileys Irish Cream (1 ounce, or 2 tablespoons, per serving)

Combine the cocoa, sugar, and salt in a large saucepan. Add the hot water and cook over medium heat, stirring all the while, until the mixture comes to a boil. Boil for 2 minutes, still stirring.

Transfer the cocoa mixture to the slow cooker, pour in the milk, and stir. Cover and heat on low for 1 hour, stirring occasionally. When the cocoa is hot, whisk in the vanilla and cinnamon. To serve, add an ounce of Baileys to each cup of cocoa. Enjoy!

Slow-Baked Potatoes

You'll need aluminum foil to get this right, but once you've tried the slow cooker method you'll never bake potatoes any other way.

YIELD: 10
PREP TIME: 5 minutes
COOK TIME: 10 hours

INGREDIENTS

10 medium russet potatoes, scrubbed and dried

toppings of choice such as sour cream, minced chives, chopped crisp bacon, and shredded cheese

Prick each potato all over with a fork. Wrap the potatoes individually in foil and place in the slow cooker.

Cover and cook on low for 10 hours. Unwrap and dress up with your favorite toppings.

St. Patrick's Day

In 1995, the Irish government started using St. Patrick's Day as an event to increase tourism. Before that? Pubs were closed on the holiday.

Party Sausages and Peppers

Serve crusty rolls or crispy fried or roasted potatoes along with these sausages.

YIELD: 6 servings
PREP TIME: 10 minutes
COOK TIME: 6 hours

INGREDIENTS

2 pounds sweet or hot Italian sausage links

2 medium onions, chopped

1 red bell pepper, seeded and cut into 2-inch pieces

2 green bell peppers, seeded and cut into 2-inch pieces

2 garlic cloves, minced

1 (14.5-ounce) can diced tomatoes, including liquid

1 (6-ounce) can tomato paste

½ cup dry red wine

1 tablespoon Italian seasoning

¼ teaspoon black pepper

¼ teaspoon salt, or more to taste

Brown the sausages in a heavy skillet over medium-high heat, turning occasionally to brown on all sides. In the slow cooker, layer half the onions and peppers. Arrange the sausages on top, then add the rest of the onions and peppers.

In the same skillet in which the sausages were browned, bring the tomatoes and juice, tomato paste, and red wine to a boil. Stir and scrape up all the browned sausage bits. Pour the mixture into the slow cooker, topping with the Italian seasoning, salt, and pepper

Cover and cook on low for 6 hours. Add salt to taste.

Traditional Guinness® Stew

This hearty dish is great for celebrating St. Patrick's Day — and for filling up a tummy before it gets filled with beer.

YIELD: 10 to 12 servings
PREP TIME: 10 to 20 minutes
COOK TIME: 8 to 10 hours

INGREDIENTS

6 medium carrots, peeled and cut into chunks

2 stalks celery, cut into chunks

8 to 10 unpeeled medium potatoes (I use yellow), cut into bite-size pieces

½ cup all-purpose flour

pinch of salt

½ teaspoon black pepper

½ teaspoon garlic powder

3 pounds boneless beef roast, cut into bite-size cubes

2 to 3 tablespoons olive oil

3 bay leaves, divided

1 medium yellow onion, minced

4 large garlic cloves, minced

11 ounces beef broth

8 ounces button mushrooms, halved

2 (8-ounce) cans tomato sauce

1 envelope onion soup mix

1 teaspoon dried thyme

1 teaspoon Creole seasoning or Emeril's Essence

1 teaspoon Italian seasoning

12 ounces (1½ cups) Guinness beer

Place the carrots, celery, and potatoes in the slow cooker and add 2 of the bay leaves. Mix the flour with the salt, pepper, and garlic powder and drag the beef cubes through the flour mixture to coat on all sides. In a medium skillet over medium heat, heat the olive oil with the remaining bay leaf. Brown the meat cubes in the oil, working in batches so you don't crowd the pan. Remove the meat from the pan and set aside.

Add the onion and garlic to the same skillet and cook for a minute or two. Then add half of the beef broth, gently scraping the sides of the skillet to deglaze the pan. Pour the contents of the skillet into the slow cooker. Add the mushrooms.

In a small bowl, mix the tomato sauce, onion soup mix, thyme, Creole seasoning, and Italian seasoning, and the remaining beef broth. Pour the mixture over the contents of the slow cooker. Finally, pour in the Guinness. (Take a sip, if you want.) Cover and cook on low for 8 to 10 hours.

Classic Corned Beef and Cabbage

A traditional St. Patrick's Day meal, this is often served on New Year's Day as well. It's just that good.

YIELD: 6 to 8 servings
PREP TIME: 15 minutes
COOK TIME: 8 hours

INGREDIENTS

10 small red-skinned potatoes

1 large onion, peeled and cut into chunks

4 cups water

4 pounds corned beef (with spice packet)

6 ounces (¾ cup) dark beer

½ head green cabbage, coarsely chopped

salt and pepper

Place the potatoes and onions in the slow cooker, pour in the water, and set the meat on top. Pour the beer over the meat and sprinkle on the contents of the spice packet that came with the corned beef.

Cover and cook on high for 8 hours. Stir, add the cabbage, and cook for 1 more hour on high. Season with salt and pepper to taste.

Potatoes au Gratin

Potatoes are always appreciated as a side for a holiday meal, and this cheesy and flavorful version is superior.

YIELD: 7 to 9 servings
PREP TIME: 20 minutes
COOK TIME: About 2 hours

INGREDIENTS

6 medium Yukon gold potatoes
3 tablespoons unsalted butter
¼ cup all-purpose flour
2 cups milk
1 tablespoon onion powder
3 cups shredded Cheddar cheese
salt

Peel and slice the potatoes, about ⅛ inch thick. Spray the slow cooker with cooking spray and add a layer of potato slices. Salt liberally. Continue layering and salting until you've used all the potatoes.

Melt the butter in a saucepan, whisk in the flour, and cook over medium heat until the mixture bubbles. Cook for about a minute more, whisking constantly. Add the milk, whisking the whole time, and stir in the onion powder. Cook until thickened. Slowly add the cheese, stirring until it's melted.

Pour the cheese mixture over the potatoes in the slow cooker, but do not stir. Cover and cook on high for 2 hours.

Easter

In Poland, men are discouraged from helping make the traditional *paska*, or Easter bread. Legend states that if the man of the house tried to make the dough it would fail to rise and his moustache would turn gray. So nobody wants him to help.

Egg Casserole

For an Easter morning treat, serve this breakfast casserole along with biscuits fresh out of the oven.

YIELD: 6 servings
PREP TIME: 10 minutes
COOK TIME: 6 to 8 hours

INGREDIENTS

10 eggs

1 cup sour cream

1 cup skim milk

1 tablespoon onion powder

1 teaspoon salt

1 teaspoon pepper

1 cup diced cooked ham

1 cup crumbled cooked sausage

1 cup crumbled cooked bacon

2 yellow bell peppers, seeded and chopped

2 cups shredded sharp Cheddar cheese

1 (4-ounce) can sliced mushrooms or 5 small button mushrooms, sliced

hot sauce or ketchup, for serving (optional)

Spray the inside of the slow cooker with cooking spray. In a bowl, whisk together the eggs, sour cream, milk, onion powder, salt, and pepper. Set aside.

Place the meats, peppers, cheese, and mushrooms in the slow cooker. Whisk the egg mixture one more time and pour it over the ingredients in the slow cooker, stirring to mix in the cheese. Cover and cook on low for 6 to 8 hours. Slice inside the slow cooker and serve with hot sauce or ketchup, if desired.

Split Pea Soup with Ham

Sometimes you just want a nice bowl of soup, and this smooth pea soup fits the bill. Use leftover Easter ham, if you have any left.

YIELD: 8 to 10 servings
PREP TIME: 10 minutes
COOK TIME: 8 to 9 hours

INGREDIENTS

1 pound dried split peas, sorted and rinsed

2 cups diced ham

½ cup diced onion

1 cup diced carrots

1 cup diced celery

2 garlic cloves, minced

1 handful fresh parsley, chopped

¼ teaspoon dried marjoram

1 bay leaf

1 teaspoon salt

½ teaspoon pepper

4 cups hot water

Place the ingredients in the slow cooker in the order in which they are listed. Cover and cook on low for 8 to 9 hours, or until the peas are soft. Stir occasionally. Remove the bay leaf and ladle the hot soup into bowls to serve.

Leg of Lamb

Your slow cooker is the easiest way to achieve a succulent, fall-off-the-bone leg of lamb.

YIELD: 8 servings
PREP TIME: 15 minutes
COOK TIME: 10 hours

INGREDIENTS

1 (5-pound) leg of lamb

5 garlic cloves, minced, divided

2 tablespoons olive oil

2 tablespoons chopped fresh rosemary

½ teaspoon chopped fresh thyme

¼ teaspoon salt

¼ teaspoon pepper

4 cups vegetable stock

¼ cup soy sauce

Use a sharp knife to make a few ½-inch cuts in the leg of lamb, and push some of the garlic into the cuts. In a small bowl, mix the olive oil with the rosemary, thyme, salt, and pepper; rub the mixture all over the meat. In a large skillet over medium-high heat, brown the leg of lamb on all sides.

Pour the stock and soy sauce into the slow cooker. Add the browned lamb, the remaining the garlic, and more salt and pepper, to taste. Cover and cook on low for 10 hours. Remove the meat from the slow cooker and let rest for 20 minutes before slicing. Serve with the cooking juices.

Honey-Glazed Ham

This traditional Easter dish is delicious and oh so easy to make in the slow cooker — leaving you plenty of time to hunt for Easter eggs.

YIELD: 16 servings
PREP TIME: 10 minutes
COOK TIME: 10 hours

EASTER

INGREDIENTS

4 to 5-pound bone-in ham, fully cooked

⅓ cup unsweetened apple juice

1 tablespoon honey

1 tablespoon spicy mustard

¼ cup firmly packed dark brown sugar

¼ teaspoon black pepper

Place the ham in the slow cooker and pour the apple juice over it. In a small bowl, mix the honey, mustard, brown sugar, and pepper. Spread liberally over the meat in the slow cooker.

Cover and cook on low for 8 hours. Remove from the slow cooker and let stand for 10 minutes before slicing.

Almond Cheesecake

Nothing tops off a great Easter dinner better than a delicious cheesecake. For this recipe, you'll need a large slow cooker (I use a round one with 7-quart capacity), a 6-inch (3-inch-deep) springform pan, and some cheesecloth.

YIELD: 8 servings
PREP TIME: 10 minutes
COOK TIME: 3 hours

INGREDIENTS

¾ cup graham cracker crumbs

2½ tablespoons unsalted butter, melted

⅔ cup plus 1 tablespoon granulated sugar, divided

¼ teaspoon ground cinnamon

¼ teaspoon salt

1 tablespoon all-purpose flour

12 ounces regular cream cheese, at room temperature

2 large eggs

1 teaspoon almond extract

1 cup sour cream

Pour water into the bottom of a large slow cooker to a depth of about 1 inch; set a rack in the bottom of the cooker. (My slow cooker came with a rack, but improvisation will work just fine.) Wrap two layers of aluminum foil around the bottom of the springform pan to ensure no water will get in while it cooks.

In a small bowl, mix the graham cracker crumbs, melted butter, 1 tablespoon of the sugar, cinnamon, and a pinch of salt. Mush the crumb mixture into a 3-inch-deep springform pan, covering the bottom and 1 inch up the sides. Set the pan on the rack in the slow cooker.

Using the paddle attachment of an electric mixer, combine the flour and remaining ⅔ cup sugar with the cream cheese and the ¼ teaspoon salt. Beat until smooth. Add the eggs and almond extract, beat until everything is blended, and add the sour cream. Beat again until well blended and smooth.

Pour the batter into the crumb-lined springform pan and set the pan on the rack in the slow cooker. Stretch a piece of cheesecloth across the top of the cooker. Cover and cook on high for 2 hours. Don't open the lid while the cheesecake is cooking! After the 2 hours, turn off the slow cooker but let the cheesecake continue to cook in it for about 1 hour longer.

Lift out the cheesecake and set it on a rack to cool for an hour or so. Cover with plastic wrap and chill in the pan for at least 5 hours before serving.

EASTER

FUN IN THE SUN

Cinco de Mayo

Mother's Day Brunch

Father's Day Sides

Fourth of July

Bastille Day

Spring and summer are times of lighthearted fun. Whether you're by the pool, at a vacation home, or in your own backyard, there's plenty to celebrate.

Beginning with Cinco de Mayo, we commemorate the Mexican army's 1862 victory over the French, and Mexican heritage in general. The slow cooker is a natural for traditional Mexican fare.

The month of May also brings us Mother's Day, often the occasion for a special brunch or tea. On Father's Day in June, Dad may be manning the grill, but the rest is up to other family members. Vegetables are at their peak for this holiday, so I've offered some great side dishes to accompany a tasty barbecue.

Although Turtle Soup was a popular delicacy in the early days of the U.S., nowadays we tend to celebrate Independence Day with a roast pig. Ten days later, French food is in order for Bastille day—French National Day—commemorating the storming of the Bastille in Paris on July 14, 1789.

Tortilla Soup

YIELD: 8 servings
PREP TIME: 30 minutes
COOK TIME: 7 hours

INGREDIENTS

1 pound boneless chicken meat (light and dark)

1 (15-ounce) can black beans, drained

10 ounces frozen corn kernels

1 (14.5-ounce) can peeled tomatoes, smashed

4 ounces chopped green chiles

1 medium yellow onion, chopped

2 garlic cloves, minced

10 ounces (1¼ cups) enchilada sauce

3 (14.5-ounce) cans chicken broth

1 teaspoon ground cumin

1 teaspoon salt

¼ teaspoon black pepper

sour cream and tortilla chips, for serving

Place everything except the sour cream and tortilla chips in the slow cooker. Cover and cook on low for 7 hours. After the 7 hours, shred the chicken in the slow cooker using two forks. Stir the soup, and it's ready to serve.

Top each serving with a dollop of sour cream and crumbled tortilla chips.

Cinco de Mayo

Looking for ways to celebrate Cinco de Mayo? The Cayman Islands hosts an air guitar competition on May 5.

Pinto Beans

Pintos make a fine side dish for a Cinco de Mayo feast, but they're also good on their own as a simple, filling meal.

YIELD: 10 servings
PREP TIME: 10 minutes (after the beans are soaked)
COOK TIME: 9 hours

INGREDIENTS

1 (1-pound) bag dried pinto beans

8 slices bacon, cut into 2-inch pieces

1 medium yellow onion, chopped

salt and pepper

Soak the beans in water overnight and then pick out any bad ones. Place the beans in the slow cooker. Add the chopped onion, then toss in the bacon pieces. Liberally season the beans with salt and pepper.

Pour water into the slow cooker to about 4 inches above the beans. Cover and cook on low for 9 hours, or until the beans are tender. Test for seasoning now and then, if you feel so inclined, and add salt and pepper as needed.

Carnitas

Carnitas are the new/old "what's hot" for Cinco de Mayo. Americans are catching on that there's more to Mexican food than ground beef. In fact, these "little meats" are much more authentic. Serve carnitas on tortillas with fresh avocado, tomatoes, and shredded queso bianco for some fabulous tacos!

YIELD: 10 servings
PREP TIME: 10 minutes
COOK TIME: 6 hours

INGREDIENTS

4 cups chicken broth, heated
1 tablespoon lime juice
2 tablespoons garlic powder
2 tablespoons onion powder
1 tablespoon ground cumin
1 tablespoon ground coriander
1 tablespoon dried oregano
½ teaspoon black pepper
¼ teaspoon salt
3-pound boneless pork butt

Mix the hot chicken broth with the lime juice and all the seasonings (garlic powder through salt); pour into the slow cooker. Set the pork butt in the liquid in the slow cooker, cover, and cook on high for 6 hours. When tender, shred and serve with tortillas and toppings.

Chicken Enchiladas

These crowd-pleasing enchiladas are full of melty, cheesy goodness — and they're super easy to make. The one advance step is baking the chicken — not difficult, and totally worth it, but it bumps up the cooking time a bit.

YIELD: 10 servings
PREP TIME: 15 minutes
COOK TIME: 6 hours

INGREDIENTS

6 boneless, skinless chicken breast halves (about 2½ pounds)

1 teaspoon onion powder

1 teaspoon chili powder

2 (10.75-ounce) cans condensed cream of chicken soup

2½ cups enchilada sauce, divided, plus more to serve

½ cup chopped yellow onion

4 ounces fresh mild chiles, chopped

18 corn tortillas

1 pound sharp Cheddar cheese, shredded

sour cream, to serve

Preheat the oven to 350°F. Rinse the chicken breasts and pat dry with paper towels. Arrange in a baking dish. Sprinkle with the onion powder and chili powder and bake uncovered for about 2 hours, or until cooked through. Shred the chicken using two forks and set aside.

In a bowl, mix the cream of chicken soup, 2 tablespoons of the enchilada sauce, the onion, and the chiles. Break the tortillas into pieces. Spray the slow cooker with cooking spray and layer tortilla pieces, chicken, sauce, and cheese up to about an inch from the top of the slow cooker. Top with a layer of enchilada sauce and more cheese. Reserve some cheese for serving.

Cook on low for 5 to 7 hours. Serve the enchiladas with sour cream, more enchilada sauce, and the rest of the shredded cheese.

Mexican Braised Beef

Serve this along with Spanish rice, or as a filling for tacos or burritos.

YIELD: 8 servings
PREP TIME: 20 minutes
COOK TIME: 6 to 8 hours

INGREDIENTS

2 large poblano peppers

2 tablespoons vegetable oil

2-pound boneless beef roast, trimmed of fat

1 medium yellow onion, cut into strips

1 garlic clove, minced

1 (14.5-ounce) can diced tomatoes, including liquid

½ cup dry red wine

½ teaspoon ground cumin

1 tablespoon minced fresh oregano

salt and pepper

Using the flame of a gas burner or a kitchen torch, blacken the peppers on all sides. Your might find it easiest to do this holding the peppers with tongs, or spearing them with a metal barbecue skewer. Wrap them together in a piece of foil and set aside.

Heat the oil in a skillet over high heat. Season the beef with salt and pepper and sear in the hot skillet, turning to sear on all sides. Remove the meat from the pan and set aside. In the same pan, cook the onion until browned. Meanwhile, take the peppers out of the foil and peel off the blackened skin. Remove the seeds, cut the peppers into strips, and add the peppers and the garlic to the pan with the onions and cook for a few minutes until softened.

Add the red wine to the skillet and stir to release any browned meat bits left in the pan. Simmer to reduce the wine by half and then add the tomatoes. Bring the mixture to a boil.

Spoon the contents of the skillet into the slow cooker and set the beef roast on top. Sprinkle with the cumin and season with salt and pepper. Cover and cook on low for 6 to 8 hours. Remove the meat, shred it with two forks and return it to the mixture in the slow cooker. Toss the mixture with the fresh oregano.

CINCO DE MAYO

Caramel Flan

Flan can be complicated to make, but the slow cooker makes it a piece of… well, flan.

YIELD: 4 servings
PREP TIME: 25 minutes
COOK TIME: 4 hours

INGREDIENTS

1½ cups granulated sugar, divided

6 eggs

1 (14-ounce) can sweetened condensed milk

3¼ cups whole milk

1 teaspoon vanilla extract

Warm a saucepan on the stovetop over medium heat then pour 1 cup of the sugar into the pan. Stir constantly until the sugar melts and browns, making caramel. Remove from the heat and spoon 3 tablespoons of the caramel into ramekins. You should be able to fit about 4 (3¼-inch or 6-ounce) ramekins into a large slow cooker. Gently rotate each ramekin until the caramel coats the sides. Set them aside.

In a bowl, whisk together the eggs, then the milks, then the remaining ½ cup of sugar, and then the vanilla, mixing everything thoroughly. For an extra-smooth flan, strain through cheesecloth. Pour the mixture over the caramel in the ramekins.

Set the ramekins in the slow cooker. Carefully add water to the slow cooker to surround the ramekins, but not enough that any will get into them. Cover and cook on high for 4 hours. Lift out the flans, let them cool on a wire rack or heatproof trivets, and then refrigerate for 1 hour. Once you remove the ramekins from the refrigerator, invert them onto plates. If the flan sticks, gently run a knife around the outer edge to dislodge it.

French Toast Casserole

This version of French toast will have brunch attendees coming back for seconds—maybe even thirds. Serve it with sage sausage or bacon to help balance the sweetness. Start your preparation the day before to let the egg mixture soak into the bread.

YIELD: 8 servings
PREP TIME: 10 minutes
COOK TIME: 3 to 4 hours

FRENCH TOAST INGREDIENTS
6 eggs
2 cups reduced-fat (2%) milk
½ teaspoon ground cinnamon
1 loaf of French bread

TOPPING INGREDIENTS
½ cup chopped nuts (some people like pecans, others prefer walnuts)
¼ cup (½ stick) unsalted butter, softened
½ cup firmly packed light brown sugar
1 teaspoon ground cinnamon
¼ teaspoon ground nutmeg

At least 6 hours ahead, whisk together the eggs, milk, and ½ teaspoon cinnamon. Tear the bread into chunks, place in a bowl, and pour the egg mixture over it. Cover with plastic wrap and refrigerate overnight.

On brunch day, spray the slow cooker with cooking spray. Pour in the bread and egg mixture. In a bowl, combine all the topping ingredients. Crumble the topping over the French toast mixture to coat the top. Cover and cook on low for 3 to 4 hours, until the top is crispy and the place smells heavenly! Spoon onto plates and pass the syrup.

Mother's Day Brunch

Mother's Day, originally known as Mother's Friendship Day, was officially declared a national holiday by Woodrow Wilson in 1914.

Breakfast Quiche

This quiche has it all — meat, cheese, potatoes, and veggies. You only need to offer hot sauce or ketchup, or serve the quiche plain with a small side of mixed fruit.

YIELD: 8 servings
PREP TIME: 10 minutes if using pre-cooked meat,
20 minutes if cooking the meat prior to assembly
COOK TIME: 12 hours

INGREDIENTS

1 (30-ounce) package shredded hash browns

1 pound sliced center-cut bacon, cooked

1 pound sage sausage, cooked

1 yellow pepper, seeded and diced

½ cup diced green onions

1½ cups sliced button mushrooms or 2 (4-ounce) cans sliced mushrooms, drained

1 pound sharp Cheddar cheese, shredded, divided

12 eggs

1 cup whole milk

¼ teaspoon dry mustard

½ teaspoon onion powder

½ teaspoon black pepper

¼ teaspoon salt

Spray your slow cooker with cooking spray. Line it with the potatoes, up the side about 1 inch, and then crumble in the bacon and add the sausage, yellow pepper, onions, mushrooms, and half the cheese.

In a bowl, beat together the eggs and the milk with a whisk or a large fork. Stir in the seasonings and pour the mixture over the ingredients in the slow cooker. Cover and cook on low for 12 hours, or until the eggs are cooked and fluffy.

Loaded Potatoes

YIELD: 4 to 6 servings
PREP TIME: 10 minutes
COOK TIME: About 9 hours

INGREDIENTS

10 small Yukon Gold potatoes, cut into bite-size pieces, peeled if you want a smoother texture

8 ounces sliced bacon, cooked and crumbled

½ cup minced fresh chives, plus more for serving

1 tablespoon onion powder

¼ teaspoon salt, plus a pinch for salting the water

¼ teaspoon black pepper

2 cups shredded Cheddar cheese (about 16 ounces)

sour cream, for serving

Soak the potato pieces in salted water for about an hour. Meanwhile, line the inside of the slow cooker with foil.

Drain the potatoes and pat dry with paper towels. Place in the foil-lined slow cooker with all the other ingredients except the cheese and sour cream. Cover and cook on low for 8 hours, until the potatoes are tender.

Sprinkle the shredded cheese over the potatoes and cook, uncovered, until the cheese is melted, about 45 minutes longer. Top with sour cream and more fresh chives to serve.

Beer Baked Beans

These flavorful baked beans make an excellent side for grilled burgers or steaks, or even barbecued chicken.

YIELD: 16 servings
PREP TIME: 20 minutes
COOK TIME: 6 hours

INGREDIENTS

8 ounces sliced center-cut bacon, cut into 1-inch pieces

1 cup diced onion

4 (15-ounce) cans pinto beans, drained

1 (15-ounce) can kidney beans, drained

1 cup barbecue sauce

¾ cup dark beer

¼ cup firmly packed light brown sugar

¼ teaspoon black pepper

Spray the slow cooker with cooking spray. Cook the bacon and onion together in a skillet until the bacon is nice and crispy. Remove the bacon and onions from the skillet and drain on a paper towel. Place all the ingredients in the slow cooker and mix well. Cover and cook on low for 6 hours.

Father's Day Sides

Father's Day was a nationally celebrated holiday as early as 1910 but wasn't formally recognized as an official national holiday until 1972.

Creamy Macaroni and Cheese

Nobody doesn't like mac and cheese! That's a double negative, but I don't care. This is the ultimate in comfort food, delicious and creamy. Who cares whether it's good for you? All things in moderation. For an extra kick, you can add diced jalapenos, bacon bits, or chives (or all three) for serving.

YIELD: 6 servings
PREP TIME: 10 minutes
COOK TIME: 6 hours

INGREDIENTS

2 eggs

1½ cups whole milk

1 (6-ounce) can evaporated milk

8 ounces uncooked elbow macaroni

2 cups shredded mild Cheddar cheese (about 16 ounces)

2 cups shredded sharp Cheddar cheese (about 16 ounces)

1 teaspoon salt

½ teaspoon black pepper

Spray the inside of the slow cooker with cooking spray. In a bowl, beat the eggs together with both milks. Stir in the macaroni and all but 1 cup of the shredded cheeses.

Pour it all into the slow cooker and top with the remaining 1 cup of shredded cheese. Add the salt and pepper, cover, and cook on low for 6 hours.

Cheesy Bacony Potatoes

Who doesn't love cheese and bacon? These potatoes make a terrific accompaniment for corned beef or pork loin. Or you can just eat them straight out of the slow cooker.

YIELD: 6 servings
PREP TIME: 10 minutes
COOK TIME: 12 hours

FATHER'S DAY SIDES

INGREDIENTS

4 medium Yukon gold potatoes, peeled and sliced as thin as possible

2 medium onions, sliced thin

4 ounces center-cut bacon, diced

1 cup shredded Cheddar cheese (about 8 ounces)

5 teaspoons unsalted butter

salt and pepper

sour cream and scallions, for serving (optional)

Line your slow cooker with enough foil to cover everything after the ingredients are added. Layer in half of the potatoes, and the onions, bacon, and cheese. Season with salt and pepper to taste and dot with half of the butter. Layer in the rest of the ingredients and dot with the remaining butter. Fold the foil over the top.

Cover and cook on low for 12 hours. To serve, top with sour cream and chopped scallions, if desired.

Crab Dip

Serve this dip with crostini toasts.

YIELD: 10 servings
PREP TIME: 10 minutes
COOK TIME: About 2 hours

INGREDIENTS

3 (8-ounce) packages reduced-fat cream cheese

½ cup prepared buffalo wing sauce

1 (10-ounce) can Rotel tomatoes with chiles, drained

½ cup whole milk

1 pound fresh claw crab meat

¼ teaspoon Old Bay Seasoning, to serve

Slowly melt the cream cheese in the slow cooker turned on low. Keep the lid off and stir often. When melted, stir in the buffalo wing sauce, Rotel tomatoes, and milk. Add the crab, stirring gently so it doesn't lose its chunkiness.

Cover and cook on low for 2 hours, stirring often (but carefully) until thoroughly mixed and warmed. Sprinkle with the Old Bay Seasoning to serve.

Fourth of July

Fireworks statistics from 2007 show that U.S. manufacturers shipped $232.3 million worth of fireworks, flares, and igniters that year.

Bourbon Bacon Baked Beans

YIELD: 6 to 8 servings
PREP TIME: Overnight, then about 35 minutes
COOK TIME: 6 to 8 hours

INGREDIENTS

4 to 6 cups dried navy beans (about 2 to 3 pounds)

6 thick slices bacon (about ½ pound)

1 cup chopped yellow onion

1 garlic clove, minced

¾ cup bourbon whiskey

¾ cup ketchup

1 teaspoon onion powder

1 cup firmly packed light brown sugar

1 teaspoon salt

Soak the beans overnight in a pot of water; drain, separating out any stones as you go. In a skillet, fry the bacon until crisp. Crumble into small pieces.

Boil the beans for 30 minutes. Drain.

Put all the ingredients in the slow cooker, cover, and cook on low for 6 to 8 hours. Check every hour or so to make sure beans are still submerged in liquid. Add water as needed. Once the beans have absorbed all the moisture and are tender, they're ready to serve.

Buffalo Chicken Wings

Wings are so hot right now. Literally. Offer these little treats along with ranch or blue cheese dressing and celery sticks.

YIELD: 24 to 48 wings, depending on size
PREP TIME: 20 minutes
COOK TIME: About 5 hours

INGREDIENTS

4 pounds chicken wings

3 tablespoons hot sauce (such as Tabasco)

1½ cups prepared buffalo wing sauce

Cut the tips off the chicken wings and discard. Separate the rest of each wing into two sections, cutting at the joint. Rinse the chicken pieces thoroughly and pat dry with paper towels. Place nonstick foil on a cookie sheet or line the sheet with foil and spray the foil with cooking spray. Place the chicken on the foil and broil for 10 minutes, turning halfway through, until the wings brown.

Stir the hot sauce into the buffalo wing sauce. Place the wings in the slow cooker and cover with the sauce, tossing the wings to coat them completely. Cover and cook on low for 5 hours, until the wings are nice and juicy.

Pulled Pork

Easy and absolutely delicious, this pulled pork is perfect for a traditional Independence Day meal.

YIELD: 6 to 8 servings
PREP TIME: 5 minutes
COOK TIME: 7 hours

INGREDIENTS

2 pounds pork tenderloin or pork shoulder

2 (8-ounce) cans V8 vegetable juice

½ cup ketchup

2 tablespoons Worcestershire sauce

½ teaspoon onion powder

½ teaspoon garlic powder

½ teaspoon black pepper

¼ teaspoon salt

¼ teaspoon chili powder

Place all the ingredients in the slow cooker, cover, and cook on low for 7 hours. That's it! Shred the meat in its juices using two forks and stir it all together.

Serve with coleslaw and BBQ sauce on a nice sesame seed bun.

BBQ Beef

Nothing says the Fourth of July like barbecue. Don't skip the liquid smoke called for in the ingredients—buy some if you don't already have it. Make up a batch of fresh coleslaw to serve with the beef.

YIELD: 6 to 8 servings
PREP TIME: 5 minutes
COOK TIME: 10 hours

INGREDIENTS

3 pounds lean boneless sirloin tip beef roast

¼ cup red wine vinegar

1½ cups ketchup

2 tablespoons spicy brown mustard

1 tablespoon Worcestershire sauce

1 teaspoon liquid smoke

¼ cup firmly packed light brown sugar

½ teaspoon garlic powder

½ teaspoon onion powder

½ teaspoon salt

¼ teaspoon black pepper

Rinse the beef, pat dry with paper towels, and place in the slow cooker. Add the rest of the ingredients. Cover and cook on low for 10 hours.

Once the roast is cooked, shred it with two forks right in the slow cooker so it can soak up the juices. Serve on a bun with coleslaw, barbecue sauce, pickles, and melted cheese.

Baked Apple Crisp

YIELD: 8 serving
PREP TIME: 5 minutes
COOK TIME: 4 hours

INGREDIENTS

¾ cup granulated sugar, divided

1 teaspoon ground cinnamon, divided

½ cup firmly packed light brown sugar, divided

¼ teaspoon ground nutmeg

½ cup (1 stick) unsalted butter, cut into pieces

1 cup all-purpose flour

6 cups Granny Smith apples, peeled, cored, and chopped into bite-size pieces

Spray the slow cooker with cooking spray. In a small bowl, mix ½ cup granulated sugar, ½ teaspoon cinnamon, ¼ cup brown sugar, and the nutmeg. Work in the butter, using a fork, until pea-sized balls have formed.

Place the cut-up apples in the bottom of the slow cooker and add all other ingredients. Cover and cook on low for 4 hours. Vent the slow cooker by tilting the lid and cook for 30 minutes longer to let the topping harden a bit.

Squash Bisque

This creamy soup can be served either warm or chilled.

YIELD: 4 servings
PREP TIME: 20 minutes
COOK TIME: 3 hours

INGREDIENTS

1 tablespoon olive oil

2½ pounds butternut squash, peeled, seeded, and cubed

2 garlic cloves, chopped

42 ounces (5¼ cups) chicken stock, strained (homemade is best, if you have it)

¾ cup heavy cream

½ tablespoon ground nutmeg

1 tablespoon ground ginger

¼ teaspoon salt

½ teaspoon black pepper

Heat the olive oil in a skillet over medium heat. Sauté the squash and garlic in the oil until soft and then transfer to the slow cooker. Add the rest of the ingredients. Purée with an immersion blender to make the mixture completely smooth. If you do not have an immersion blender, transfer the mixture to a traditional blender or food processer and purée. Return mixture to slow cooker and cover and cook on low for 3 hours.

Serve warm, or refrigerate to serve chilled.

Bastille Day

Paris commemorates Bastille Day every year with a parade on the Champs-Elysées.

Ratatouille

With this dish, it's very easy to eat your vegetables.

YIELD: 8 servings
PREP TIME: 30 minutes
COOK TIME: 3½ hours

INGREDIENTS

1 small eggplant, peeled and cubed

1 red bell pepper, seeded and cubed

1 yellow bell pepper, seeded and cubed

1 medium yellow onion, cut into chunks

1 (14.5-ounce) can diced tomatoes, including juices

1 (8-ounce) can no-salt-added tomato sauce

½ teaspoon Italian seasoning

1½ teaspoons salt

¾ teaspoon black pepper

1 medium yellow squash, peeled (optional) and cubed

1 medium yellow zucchini, peeled (optional) and cubed

1 tablespoon chopped fresh basil

2 tablespoons olive oil

Place the first nine ingredients (eggplant through black pepper) in the slow cooker. Stir. Cook on high for 3 hours. Add the squash and zucchini and cook another 30 minutes.

To serve, toss with the basil and drizzle with olive oil.

Boeuf en Daube

French, fabulous, and fun to make.

YIELD: 8 to 12 servings
PREP TIME: 1 hour
COOK TIME: About 6 hours

BASTILLE DAY

INGREDIENTS

2 teaspoons olive oil

12 garlic cloves, crushed

2 pounds boneless chuck roast, trimmed of fat and cut into 1-inch cubes

1 cup dry red wine

2 cups chopped carrots

1½ cups chopped onions

1 (14.5-ounce) can diced tomatoes with liquid

½ cup beef broth

1 teaspoon tomato paste

1½ teaspoons salt

½ teaspoons black pepper

1 teaspoon chopped fresh rosemary

1 teaspoon chopped fresh thyme

1 bay leaf

In a Dutch oven or other stew pot, heat the oil and sauté the garlic in it. Remove the garlic once it's soft and set it aside.

Add the beef cubes to the pan and brown on all sides, seasoning with salt and pepper while they are browning. Remove the beef and set it aside, covered. Pour the wine into the Dutch oven and bring it to a boil. Make sure you scrape the bottom and sides of the pot to get all those meaty bits. Add all the other ingredients and bring to a boil.

Pour the mixture into the slow cooker over the beef and cook on high for 5½ hours.

Chicken Provençal Stew

Simple but delicious, this meal is a breeze to make in the slow cooker—and wonderful as leftovers. I've even eaten it cold.

YIELD: 4 to 6 servings
PREP TIME: 20 minutes
COOK TIME: 8 to 10 hours

INGREDIENTS

¼ cup olive oil

8 chicken pieces (breasts, thighs, legs), skin removed

¼ teaspoon salt

¼ teaspoon black pepper

4 garlic cloves, shaved

1 yellow bell pepper, seeded and cut into strips

1 orange bell pepper, seeded and cut into strips

2 medium yellow onions, sliced thin

1 (14.5-ounce) can diced tomatoes with juices

1 cup pitted green olives

½ cup dry white wine

2 tablespoons herbs de Provence

Rub the inside of the slow cooker with the olive oil. Place the chicken pieces in the slow cooker and season them with the salt and pepper. Add the rest of the ingredients, saving the herbs de Provence to sprinkle on last.

Cover and cook on low for 8 to 10 hours.

Coq Au Vin

A classic French dish, chicken with wine is a must for any French-style celebration. Using the slow cooker cuts out some of the usual complicated preparation, but not all, so you'll feel like a gourmet when you serve this up to your guests.

YIELD: 4 to 6 servings
PREP TIME: 45 minutes
COOK TIME: 6 hours

INGREDIENTS

3 tablespoons unbleached all-purpose flour

4 boneless, skinless chicken thighs

2 boneless, skinless chicken breasts, and cut into thirds

6 slices center-cut bacon, chopped into 1-inch pieces

3 tablespoons unsalted butter, divided

12 ounces button mushrooms, halved

3 carrots, peeled and chopped into 1-inch pieces

1 medium yellow onion, chopped into large pieces

2 garlic cloves, crushed

½ cup chicken stock (homemade is best, if you have it)

1½ cups dry red wine

2 teaspoons dried thyme

1 cup flour

salt and pepper

Season the flour with salt and pepper and dredge the chicken pieces through it. Set aside to bring the chicken to room temperature.

Cook the bacon in a skillet over medium to medium-high heat until just barely crisp and remove from the pan. Drain the bacon fat and melt 2 tablespoons butter in the skillet. Cook the chicken pieces in the skillet until brown on all sides; set aside.

Melt the remaining 1 tablespoon butter in the same skillet; add the mushrooms, carrots, onion, and garlic. Cook until the vegetables have soaked up the butter and begin to soften. Transfer them to the slow cooker, pour in the stock, place the chicken on top, and add the bacon.

Pour the wine over everything and sprinkle on the thyme. Season with and salt and pepper. Cover and cook on low for 6 hours, or until the sauce thickens and the chicken is very tender.

FALL CELEBRATIONS

Autumn is a time for hearty meals and aromatic desserts as we welcome cooler weather. The recipes in this chapter will get the fall festivities rolling and see you through Thanksgiving, putting your trusty slow cooker to work while you spend your time doing craft projects, watching scary movies, or just watching the leaves fall.

Starting in late September, Oktoberfest celebrates Bavarian culture. Roast meats and sausages are popular — along with beer, of course. For Halloween at the end of October, candy may be the food of choice for the youngsters, but adults (and kids, too) will enjoy filling stews and scrumptious desserts.

Then comes Thanksgiving. The meal we're familiar with today is a little different from the first Thanksgiving dinner celebrated by the Pilgrims in 1621 at Plymouth. That meal was a smorgasbord of salted and fresh fish, venison, root vegetables, and some fowl (including wild turkey). Today's Thanksgiving feast traditionally includes turkey, potatoes, cranberries, and pumpkin pie — in keeping with the spirit of the autumn harvest season.

Kielbasa and Kraut

You couldn't ask for a tastier accompaniment for some great Oktoberfest beer. Serve this traditional German dish with fresh, crusty bread.

YIELD: 8 servings
PREP TIME: 20 minutes
COOK TIME: 6 hours

INGREDIENTS

2 pounds kielbasa sausage

1 tablespoon olive oil

1 medium yellow onion, sliced

4 cups prepared sauerkraut

1 cup water

1 cup apple cider (not apple juice)

Slice the sausage in 1-inch slices; set aside. In a skillet, heat the oil over medium heat. Add the onion and cook, stirring occasionally, until caramelized. Drain the sauerkraut, squeezing out all the moisture you can.

Place everything in the slow cooker, cover, and cook on high for 6 hours.

Oktoberfest

The 2004 Munich Oktoberfest generated 978 tons of trash.

Oktoberfest Short Ribs

These tender, fall-off-the-bone short ribs are a great complement to Oktoberfest parties and taste great with a side of fried potatoes.

YIELD: 6 servings
PREP TIME: 25 minutes
COOK TIME: About 8 hours

INGREDIENTS

4 tablespoons all-purpose flour, divided

¼ teaspoon salt

¼ teaspoon pepper

3 pounds beef short ribs

2 tablespoons olive oil

1 large yellow onion, sliced

½ cup dry red wine

1 tablespoon Worcestershire sauce

3 tablespoons cider vinegar

3 tablespoons light brown sugar

½ teaspoon chili powder

½ teaspoon dry mustard

Season 2 tablespoons of the flour with the salt and pepper. Coat the short ribs with the flour. Heat the olive oil in a skillet over medium-high heat and brown the ribs on all sides.

Mix together all the other ingredients (red wine through dry mustard) in the slow cooker, then add the short ribs. Cover and cook on low for 8 hours. Remove the ribs from the slow cooker and cover with foil to keep warm.

Turn the slow cooker temperature to high and stir in the remaining 2 tablespoons flour. Cover and cook another 15 minutes, until the sauce is thickened. Pass the sauce to serve with the ribs.

Halloween Pumpkin Soup

YIELD: 6 to 8 servings
PREP TIME: 15 minutes
COOK TIME: 6 hours

INGREDIENTS

1 (15-ounce) can canned pumpkin

1 medium yellow onion, chopped

2 cups frozen corn kernels

4 garlic cloves, minced

½ cup toasted pine nuts

½ cup grated Parmesan cheese, plus more for garnish

42 ounces (5¼ cups) chicken broth

2 cups half-and-half

¼ teaspoon black pepper

½ teaspoon salt

cilantro, for garnish

Place all the ingredients in the slow cooker and stir to combine. Cook on low for 6 hours. Stir occasionally and ladle into bowls. Garnish with grated Parmesan or fresh cilantro.

Halloween

The tradition of carving a jack-o'-lantern comes to us from the Irish. In Ireland, jack-o'-lanterns made from hollowed-out gourds were placed in windows to scare away a legendary character named Stingy Jack.

Perfect Wild Rice Pilaf

This rice is perfect as a side dish for your Halloween dinner and complements stews nicely. Be sure to use cooking spray to keep the rice from sticking to the cooker.

YIELD: 6 servings
PREP TIME: 15 minutes
COOK TIME: 3 hours

INGREDIENTS

2 cups uncooked wild rice

½ cup finely chopped sweet onion

½ teaspoon salt

1 teaspoon black pepper

14 ounces (1¾ cups) chicken broth

½ cup water

1 teaspoon dried thyme

4 ounces sliced button mushrooms (optional)

Spray your slow cooker with nonstick cooking spray. Rinse the rice and drain completely.

Place the uncooked rice in the slow cooker together with the onion, salt, pepper, chicken broth, water, thyme, and mushrooms, if using. *Stir the mixture thoroughly.* Cover and cook on high for 3 hours, until the rice is completely cooked.

Autumn Pork Stew

A hearty dish to serve to your hungry trick-or-treaters, this is also delicious with fall beer for the grown-ups who accompany them.

YIELD: 4 to 6 servings
PREP TIME: 20 minutes
COOK TIME: 8 hours

INGREDIENTS

6 medium Yukon gold potatoes, quartered (optionally peeled)

1 medium yellow onion, cut into chunks

1 pound carrots, peeled and cut into medallions

2 garlic cloves, chopped

2-pound boneless pork roast, trimmed

1¾ cups chicken stock (homemade is best, if you have it)

1 teaspoon dried thyme

½ teaspoon dry mustard

1 teaspoon salt

½ teaspoon black pepper

Place the potatoes, onion, carrots, and garlic in the slow cooker; top with the pork roast. Pour in the chicken stock. Add the thyme, mustard, salt, and pepper.

Cover and cook on low for 8 hours, as the delicious aroma fills your house.

Remove the roast and let rest before slicing. Serve with the juices and vegetables.

S'more Fondue

Here's a treat that will keep the kids from diving into their candy right away.

YIELD: 8 to 10 servings
PREP TIME: 15 minutes
COOK TIME: 2 hours

INGREDIENTS

15 ounces milk chocolate
10 ounces large marshmallows
½ cup half-and-half
graham crackers, for dipping

Stir the chocolate, marshmallows, and half-and-half together in the slow cooker. Cover and heat on low for 1 hour. Stir once, cover again, and cook 1 hour more.

Whisk to make a smooth fondue. To make it an authentic s'more experience, use graham crackers to scoop up this yummy dessert.

Silky Smooth Sweet Potato Purée

For this one, you're cooking the potatoes in the slow cooker, then puréeing them and returning them to the slow cooker. That frees up oven space and keeps the dish warm. Perfect!

YIELD: 8 servings
PREP TIME: 30 minutes
COOK TIME: 6 hours

INGREDIENTS

5 medium sweet potatoes or yams, unpeeled (about 1½ pounds)

½ cup whole milk

½ cup buttermilk

6 tablespoons (¾ stick) unsalted butter, softened

salt and pepper

grated nutmeg

Scrub the sweet potatoes thoroughly, but don't dry them. Using a fork or skewer, poke several holes in each potato. Place in the slow cooker and sprinkle with salt and pepper. Cover and cook on high for about 6 hours. (That gives you plenty of time to concentrate on the rest of the menu!)

Remove the potatoes from the slow cooker, peel, and cut into cubes. Transfer the chunks into the bowl of a food processor and add salt and pepper to taste. Purée the potatoes, slowly adding the whole milk, then the buttermilk, and finally the butter through the processor's feeder tube. Make sure everything is well puréed and combined, but don't let the mixture liquefy.

Spoon the potato mixture back into the slow cooker, sprinkle with nutmeg to taste, set the slow cooker on warm — and wait for the oohs and ahs.

Thanksgiving

In sixteenth-century England, Queen Elizabeth I is said to have eaten roast goose at harvest festival time. When British settlers came to America, the closest they could come was the abundant wild turkey. Thus began the significance of the turkey for festival celebrations.

Buttery Mashed Potatoes

This is a multistep recipe, but you'll end up with the yummiest mashed potatoes ever.

YIELD: 8 servings
PREP TIME: 15 minutes
COOK TIME: 4 hours

INGREDIENTS

16 medium to large Yukon Gold potatoes

3 tablespoons unsalted butter

1½ cups heavy cream

½ teaspoon salt

½ teaspoon black pepper

Using a fork or skewer, poke holes in the potatoes so they won't explode while cooking. Wrap the potatoes individually in foil and place in the slow cooker. Cover and cook on high for 4 hours.

Remove the cooked potatoes and set the slow cooker on warm. Unwrap each potato and peel off the skin. In a small saucepan over medium-high heat, heat the butter and cream together; do not scald or boil.

Force the potatoes through a ricer directly into the slow cooker. (If you don't have a ricer, use a potato masher to mash vigorously.) Pour in the cream and butter mixture, stir well, and you've made some deliciously creamy mashed potatoes. The slow cooker will keep them warm all the way to the plate.

Classic Green Bean Casserole

Now you can have this Thanksgiving favorite without any hassle or fuss.

YIELD: 6 servings
PREP TIME: 15 minutes
COOK TIME: 7 hours

THANKSGIVING

INGREDIENTS

1 (14.5-ounce) can cut green beans, drained

1 (14.5-ounce) can French-style green beans, drained

2 (4-ounce) cans mushroom pieces, drained, or 1 cup sliced button mushrooms

1½ cup fresh pearl onions

1 (10.5-ounce) can condensed cream of mushroom soup

½ cup reduced fat (2%) milk

½ teaspoon Worcestershire sauce

½ teaspoon black pepper

½ teaspoon salt

Coat the slow cooker with cooking spray. Pour in both kinds of green beans, the mushrooms, and the onions; mix together.

In a bowl, stir together the soup, milk, Worcestershire, pepper, and salt. Pour over the beans, but don't stir. Cook on low for 7 hours.

Sweet Potato Casserole

YIELD: 8 servings
PREP TIME: 15 minutes
COOK TIME: 3 hours

POTATO INGREDIENTS

2 medium sweet potatoes or yams, peeled and cooked (about 1 pound)

2 tablespoons granulated sugar

2 tablespoons light brown sugar

⅓ cup melted unsalted butter, melted

1 tablespoon orange juice

½ cup low-fat (1%) milk

2 eggs, beaten

TOPPING INGREDIENTS

⅓ cup firmly packed light brown sugar

2 teaspoons unsalted butter, melted

2 tablespoons unbleached all-purpose flour

⅓ cup chopped pecans (optional)

To make the potatoes, spray the slow cooker with cooking spray. In a bowl, combine the sweet potatoes, granulated sugar, brown sugar, and melted butter. Break the sweet potatoes into chunks and mash. Beat in the orange juice, milk, and eggs. Leave the mixture somewhat chunky. Transfer the mixture to the slow cooker.

To make the topping, in a small bowl, mix the ingredients until well combined. Top the sweet potato mixture in the slow cooker with the topping, but do not stir. Cook on high for 3 hours; serve hot.

Heavenly Squash and Apples

Squash and apples pair beautifully to make healthy and tasty side dish for a Thanksgiving feast.

YIELD: 8 servings
PREP TIME: 10 minutes
COOK TIME: 5 hours

INGREDIENTS

1 (4-pound) butternut squash, peeled, seeded, and cut into 1-inch cubes

4 Granny Smith apples, cored, peeled, and chopped

½ medium sweet onion, diced

1 tablespoon ground cinnamon

1½ teaspoons ground nutmeg

1 teaspoon ground allspice

Combine the squash, apples, onion, and spices in the slow cooker. Cover and cook on high for 5 hours, stirring at least once an hour while cooking.

Cornbread Dressing

I use store-bought cornbread from the specialty bread department for this recipe. In other words, I use cornbread that I like, but I don't go to the trouble of making it from scratch.

YIELD: 14 to 16 servings
PREP TIME: 15 minutes
COOK TIME: 4 hours

INGREDIENTS

6 cups crumbled cooked cornbread

8 slices slightly stale white or wheat bread, left out overnight to dry

4 eggs, beaten

¾ cup finely chopped celery

1 medium yellow onion, finely chopped

1½ tablespoons herb mixture of sage, thyme, celery salt, and seasoning salt (poultry seasoning)

½ teaspoon black pepper

2 (10.75-ounce) cans condensed reduced-sodium cream of chicken soup

21 ounces (about 2½ cups) turkey broth or chicken broth

⅛ teaspoon salt

¼ cup (½ stick) unsalted butter

Spray the slow cooker with cooking spray. Crumble the cornbread and dried sliced bread together in a bowl. Mix in all the other ingredients except for the butter. Pour the mixture into the slow cooker.

Dot the top with the butter, cover, and cook on low for 4 hours. You'll have a cornbread stuffing that tastes like you spent hours cooking it. (And you did — in the slow cooker.)

Easy Turkey Breast

This turkey is so simple to prepare that you'll find it hard to believe how good it tastes.

YIELD: 12 servings
PREP TIME: 15 minutes
COOK TIME: 7 to 8 hours

THANKSGIVING

INGREDIENTS

1 (6-pound) turkey breast
(preferably bone-in)

1 envelope onion soup mix

½ cup water

Thoroughly rinse the turkey breast and pat dry with paper towels. Rub the soup mix all over the turkey, working it up under the skin.

Place the turkey breast in your slow cooker. Cover and cook on high for 1 hour and then remove the lid; if the turkey looks overly brown, add a little of the water. Cover again and cook on high for another 6 to 7 hours, adding water as necessary.

Savory Stuffed Cornish Game Hens

These juicy little birds are big on flavor! We opt to stuff them, so all you need to add are some veggies and you've got yourself a complete meal.

YIELD: 4 servings
PREP TIME: 15 minutes
COOK TIME: 5 to 7 hours

INGREDIENTS

4 Cornish game hens (thawed, if frozen)

1 teaspoon salt

1 teaspoon black pepper

8 ounces packaged stuffing mix

1½ teaspoons vegetable oil
1 tablespoon fresh-squeezed lemon juice

1 cup chicken stock (homemade is best, if you have it)

2 tablespoons flour

water

Thoroughly rinse the hens inside and out and pat dry with paper towels. Salt and pepper both the outside and the inside.

Prepare the stuffing according to the package instructions. Spoon it into the hens and truss them closed with cooking twine. If you have stuffing left over, form it into balls, top each one with a whole pecan, and pop in a 375°F oven for about 30 minutes or until cooked through.

Place the birds in your slow cooker, neck down, and drizzle on the vegetable oil and lemon juice. Pour the chicken stock over the birds.

Cook for 5 to 7 hours on low, basting with the juices several times during cooking. Serve with the juices or make gravy.

To make gravy, transfer the juices to a saucepan over medium-high heat. In a small bowl, mix the flour with just enough water to make a smooth mixture and season with salt and pepper. Whisk the flour mixture into the saucepan and bring to a boil, whisking vigorously until smooth and thickened.

Easy Tender Turkey Legs

Maybe you're planning a small Thanksgiving dinner. Or maybe your turkey's two legs just aren't enough for your family and you want extras. Maybe you simply want a taste of Thanksgiving in spring or summer. Whatever your reason for doing so, preparing turkey legs in the slow cooker takes little effort and results in fall-off-the-bone goodness.

YIELD: 4 to 6 servings
PREP TIME: 10 minutes
COOK TIME: 7 to 8 hours

INGREDIENTS

4 to 6 turkey legs, skin removed

2 tablespoons olive oil

1 tablespoon dried rosemary

1 tablespoon dried oregano

1 tablespoon dried thyme

2 teaspoons seasoning mixture of equal parts paprika, onion powder, and salt

½ cup chicken broth

½ teaspoon black pepper

Spray your slow cooker's meat rack with cooking spray. If you don't have a rack for your slow cooker, improvise with a rack that fits, or use aluminum foil. Brush the turkey legs with the olive oil. In a small bowl, mix together the rosemary, oregano, and thyme. Rub half the herb and seasoning mixtures on the turkey legs and brown each side ever so slightly in a skillet over medium-high heat. Transfer the turkey legs to the slow cooker.

Add the broth and the remaining herb and seasoning mixtures, and the black pepper. Cover and cook on low for 8 to 9 hours or longer, depending on the size and number of legs. (If you're cooking 6 large legs, they may take 10 hours to cook through.) You'll know they're ready when the meat pretty much falls off the bone.

Turkey Soup with Dumplings

A great alternative to a traditional Thanksgiving meal, this yummy soup will satisfy and sticks to your ribs. If you're a traditionalist as far as your Thanksgiving Day menu, you can use the turkey carcass from that dinner for this recipe. You'll want to use a slow cooker liner for this dish.

YIELD: 10 to 12 servings
PREP TIME: 5 minutes, then 15 minutes for dumplings
COOK TIME: 7 to 10 hours

SOUP INGREDIENTS
1 turkey carcass, chopped up
8 cups water
1 (10-ounce) can whole tomatoes
4 chicken bullion cubes
½ cup diced carrots
1 cup diced celery
1 cup chopped onion
½ cup chopped parsley
1 bay leaf

DUMPLING INGREDIENTS
1½ cups unbleached all-purpose flour
2 teaspoons baking powder
¾ teaspoon salt
2 teaspoons dried parsley
½ teaspoon dried rosemary
3 tablespoons shortening
¾ cup whole milk

Place all the soup ingredients in the slow cooker. Cover and cook on low for 7 to 10 hours. Lift out the turkey pieces, separating the meat from the bones and returning it to the slow cooker. Discard the bones, skin, and cartilage.

For the dumplings, mix the flour, baking powder, salt, parsley, and rosemary together in a bowl. Cut in the shortening until the mixture looks like a coarse meal. Add enough of the milk to moisten the mixture without thinning the batter. Using a spoon, scoop the mixture into 1½-inch-diameter mounds and drop into the soup. Keep the dumplings spaced apart.

Cover and cook on high for 20 minutes. Remove the lid, lift out the dumplings, and place them in a serving bowl. Ladle the hot soup over the dumplings to serve in individual bowls.

Sweet and Easy Cranberry Sauce

You can make this sauce a day ahead, leaving one less task for Thanksgiving Day.

YIELD: 4 to 6 servings
PREP TIME: 10 minutes
COOK TIME: 3 hours

INGREDIENTS

4 cups fresh or frozen cranberries

½ cup water

1 cup sugar

1 teaspoon lemon juice

Mix the cranberries, sugar, water, and lemon juice in the slow cooker. Cover and cook on high for 3 hours, or until the cranberries burst. Transfer to a bowl and refrigerate for at least 2 hours, or up to 18 hours.

Pumpkin Butter

Who says pumpkin has to be reserved for pie? Make this delicious butter to spread on fresh bread, muffins, or even sweet potatoes. Use canned pumpkin purée, or make it yourself if you want a more homemade touch.

YIELD: About 50 servings
PREP TIME: 5 minutes
COOK TIME: 6 hours

THANKSGIVING

INGREDIENTS

8 cups pumpkin purée (not pumpkin pie filling)

4 cups granulated sugar

2 teaspoons ground cinnamon

1 teaspoon ground ginger

½ teaspoon ground cloves

¼ teaspoon ground nutmeg

2 lemons

½ cup water

Mix together the pumpkin purée, sugar, and spices (cinnamon through nutmeg). Squeeze the juice of the lemons into the mixture and then stir in the water. Spoon the mixture into the slow cooker.

Cover and cook on low until smooth and thick, about 6 hours. Let cool, then refrigerate for at least 6 hours.

Pumpkin Custard

Cooked in individual ramekins, these custards make for an elegant dessert presentation.

YIELD: 4 to 6 servings, depending on the size of your ramekins
PREP TIME: 20 minutes
COOK TIME: 4 to 4½ hours

INGREDIENTS

3 eggs

3 cups pumpkin purée (not pumpkin pie filling)

1 cup condensed milk

½ cup granulated sugar

½ teaspoon ground cinnamon

¼ teaspoon ground nutmeg

¼ teaspoon ground allspice

Line the slow cooker with foil, crossing sheets so that you will be able to use the foil to lift out the custards when they are done cooking.

In a bowl, beat the eggs slightly and combine with the pumpkin, condensed milk, sugar, cinnamon, nutmeg, and allspice. Whisk it all together and pour into 4 to 6 ramekins, depending on the size of ramekin and the size of your slow cooker. Cover each ramekin tightly with foil. Set the ramekins in the foil-lined slow cooker. If you have mixture left over, pour it into a baking dish and pop it in the over for 1 hour at 325°F.

Pour water into the slow cooker until the ramekins are surrounded but no water gets into them. Cook on low for 4 to 4½ hours, until a knife inserted into the custard comes out clean. Carefully lift out the foil strips to remove the hot ramekins.

HAPPY HOLIDAYS

The winter holiday season is a special time, with families gathering together and everyone (hopefully) filled with good cheer — and, let's not forget, good food. Using a slow cooker to make some of the dishes on your menus can be a lifesaver. That oven is only so big, after all.

While some traditional dishes were part of English Christmas feasts as far back as the 1600s, I'm suggesting a few different options. After years of cooking turkey for Thanksgiving and then again a month later for Christmas, I finally got tired of it! I've cooked each of the dishes in this chapter at Christmas, and I can tell you that they are equally as satisfying as Thanksgiving Dinner Part II, aka the traditional Christmas dinner.

For Hanukkah it's a bit trickier. I'm going to be honest: it's not easy to fix Hanukkah meals in the slow cooker. But there are a couple of dishes that you can make in a slow cooker to give yourself more time and stovetop space for those labor-intensive latkes and cheese blintzes.

Creamy Scalloped Potatoes

Scalloped potatoes are a comfort food that complements ham, turkey, beef, or lamb. This version is a little healthier than most. Of course, you can substitute "the real thing" for the low-sodium and low-fat ingredients, if you prefer.

YIELD: 10 to 12 servings
PREP TIME: 15 minutes
COOK TIME: About 3 hours

INGREDIENTS

12 medium Yukon gold potatoes

¼ cup chopped sweet onion

1 (10.75-ounce) can low-sodium condensed cream of chicken soup

1 cup reduced-fat sour cream

½ cup (1 stick) unsalted butter

1 cup shredded reduced-fat Cheddar cheese (I like white Cheddar)

1 teaspoon salt

½ teaspoon freshly ground black pepper

crumbled cooked bacon, for topping (optional)

Peel the potatoes and slice about ⅛ inch thick. Cook in boiling water for 3 minutes or so and then drain. Mix the potatoes with all the other ingredients except the bacon and place in the slow cooker.

Cover and cook on high for 3 hours. Serve with crumbled bacon to sprinkle on top, if you'd like.

Christmas

In Britain, flaming pudding is a longstanding Christmas tradition, baked full of coins or tokens for children to find. The pudding is made weeks in advance, and the idea is for family members to take turns stirring—making wishes as they do so.

If you celebrate Christmas in North Carolina, you may encounter Moravian love feast buns, made with flour and mashed potatoes. In Virginia, oyster and ham pie might be on the menu. A New Mexico Christmas isn't complete without empanaditas—beef pies made with raisins and pine nuts. Hawaii celebrates fire pit–style with turkey teriyaki cooked outdoors.

Southern whiskey cakes, a holiday tradition, contain a whole cup of 100-proof whiskey.

Brussels Sprouts with Spicy Brown Mustard

If you're one of those people who never thought you'd meet a Brussels sprout you liked, this recipe will make you think again. These guys are tasty, tender, and oh so good for you.

YIELD: 6 servings
PREP TIME: 10 minutes
COOK TIME: 4 hours

INGREDIENTS

1 pound fresh Brussels sprouts

3 tablespoons unsalted butter, melted

1 tablespoon spicy brown mustard

¼ teaspoon kosher salt

¼ teaspoon cracked black pepper

¼ cup water

Trim the stem ends and cut the Brussels sprouts in half. Place in the slow cooker and pour the butter over them. Mix in the remaining ingredients. Cover and cook on low for 4 hours, stirring well before serving. The Brussels sprouts along the edge of the slow cooker should get crispy. Yum!

Candied Sweet Potatoes

Super easy, and so sweet and flavorful.

YIELD: 6 to 8 servings
PREP TIME: 15 minutes
COOK TIME: 7 hours

INGREDIENTS

5 large peeled sweet potatoes or yams, cubed

1 cup firmly packed light brown sugar

juice and zest of 1 orange

¼ cup honey, local if possible

4 teaspoons unsalted butter

½ teaspoon vanilla extract

1½ teaspoons ground cinnamon

Spray the slow cooker with cooking spray. Place the cubed sweet potatoes in the slow cooker.

Combine all the other ingredients in a saucepan and heat over medium heat, stirring, until blended. Pour the mixture over the sweet potato cubes in the slow cooker. Cover and cook on low for 7 hours, or until the potatoes are soft all the way through.

Hearty Root Vegetable Stew

Great as a main dish, as a side, or doctored up with breadcrumbs as a casserole, these root vegetables are filling, delicious, and vegan. It's best to cook down the onions and season them prior to putting the stew together.

YIELD: 10 to 12 servings
PREP TIME: 5 minutes
COOK TIME: 3½ hours

INGREDIENTS

¼ cup olive oil

2 medium yellow onions, cut in large dice

2 pinches kosher salt (about ½ teaspoon)

¼ teaspoon ground cumin

⅛ teaspoon cayenne pepper

2 pinches freshly ground black pepper (about ¼ teaspoon)

1 pound Yukon Gold potatoes, cut in large dice (about 3 large)

1 pound carrots, peeled and cut in large dice (about 4 or 5 medium)

1 pound parsnips, peeled and cut in large dice (about 4 medium)

3 cups low-sodium chicken or vegetable broth

1½ tablespoons cider vinegar, plus more as needed

handful of fresh parsley, coarsely chopped, for garnish

Heat the oil in a skillet over medium heat and throw in the onions, a pinch of salt, and the cumin, cayenne pepper, and a sprinkling of black pepper. Cook over medium heat until the onions are translucent.

Transfer to the slow cooker and cover with the potatoes, carrots, parsnips, and broth. Sprinkle on more salt and pepper. Cover and cook on high for 3½ hours, stirring occasionally. Stir in the vinegar and taste; add vinegar, salt, and pepper as needed, to taste.

To serve, sprinkle the stew with the chopped parsley.

Christmas Lamb Roast

If a Christmas lamb is your thing, here's a recipe that literally couldn't get any easier. The only extra step is browning the roast in a skillet to seal the flavor in.

YIELD: 7 to 9 servings
PREP TIME: 20 minutes
COOK TIME: About 7 to 8 hours

CHRISTMAS

INGREDIENTS

1 (4-pound) lamb rib roast

4 tablespoons cooking oil (canola or other vegetable oil is fine)

½ teaspoon salt

½ teaspoon pepper

1 tablespoon chopped fresh rosemary

Using a sharp knife, remove the thin outer layer of the lamb roast (called the fell). Heat the oil in a heavy skillet until it is very hot, then sear the roast in the hot oil. Make sure you sear all sides—you want it to be nice and brown all over.

Sprinkle the salt, pepper, and rosemary on all sides of the meat. It helps to put all the seasonings on a paper plate and roll the roast around in them to coat it all over.

Place the meat in the slow cooker, cover, and cook on low for 7 to 8 hours, until the roast reaches an internal temperature of 150°F. Take the roast out of the slow cooker and let it rest, covered, for 15 minutes before slicing it.

Maple Brown Sugar Ham

Ham is extra succulent and delicious prepared in the slow cooker. I use dark brown sugar for the richest flavor and color. Discard the flavor packet that comes with the ham. Note: If you have a small slow cooker, get a smaller ham and reduce the amount of other ingredients as needed. This recipe uses a 6-quart slow cooker.

YIELD: 24 servings
PREP TIME: 5 minutes
COOK TIME: 5 hours

INGREDIENTS

1 cup firmly packed dark brown sugar

1 (8-pound) bone-in, spiral-cut ham

½ cup real maple syrup

2 cups pineapple juice

Set the ham (unwrapped and sans flavor packet) flat side down in a large slow cooker. Rub the brown sugar all over it and pour on the maple syrup and pineapple juice. Cover and cook for 5 hours, basting with the liquid in the cooker after 4 hours.

When the ham is thoroughly heated, remove it from the slow cooker and let it rest, covered in foil, for 10 to 20 minutes before slicing.

Succulent Beef Tenderloin

Beef tenderloin is an excellent alternative to ham or turkey for Christmas dinner. Remember, the better the meat, the more flavorful and tender it will be — don't be afraid to splurge.

YIELD: 6 to 8 servings
PREP TIME: 20 minutes
COOK TIME: About 10 hours

INGREDIENTS

4 tablespoons cooking oil

3 pounds beef tenderloin, trimmed

1 teaspoon chopped fresh rosemary

freshly ground black pepper

4 garlic cloves

1 to 2 teaspoons kosher salt

1 cup water, as needed

Heat the oil in a skillet. Sear the tenderloin on all sides in the hot oil — this helps seal in the flavor. Place the tenderloin in the slow cooker and season with the rosemary and pepper to taste. Season liberally with the salt, starting with 1 teaspoon and increasing to taste. Poke the garlic cloves into the meat.

Cover and cook on low for 10 hours, adding water if the meat starts to look dry. Remove the tenderloin and let it rest, covered in foil, for 20 minutes before slicing.

Sugar-Baked Apples

Baked apples are great to serve in lieu of a pie, and they're a crowd-pleaser. Serve this classic dessert with ice cream, if you're so inclined.

YIELD: 5 servings
PREP TIME: 10 minutes
COOK TIME: 7 hours

INGREDIENTS

1 small box raisins (about ½ tablespoon per apple)

2 cups firmly packed light brown sugar (you may not need all of it)

1½ teaspoons ground cinnamon

½ teaspoon ground nutmeg

5 apples

5 teaspoons unsalted butter

In a small bowl, mix together the raisins, brown sugar, cinnamon, and nutmeg. Start with 1 cup brown sugar, and adjust the amount to taste.

Core the apples and peel the tops to about an inch down the side. Set the apples into the slow cooker, core side up, and fill with the sugar and spice mixture. For more flavor, don't be afraid to pack it in with your finger.

Top each apple with a pat of butter. Cover and cook on low for 7 hours, until the apples are nice and tender.

Cinnamon Bread Pudding

YIELD: 7 to 9 servings
PREP TIME: 5 minutes
COOK TIME: 4 to 5 hours

INGREDIENTS

5 eggs, beaten

3½ cups milk

2 teaspoons vanilla extract

½ teaspoon salt

2 tablespoons ground cinnamon

6 cups plain dry breadcrumbs or shredded stale bread

¾ cup firmly packed light brown sugar

1 tablespoon unsalted butter, melted

½ cup golden raisins

Spray the slow cooker thoroughly with cooking spray. Stir all the ingredients together so that the breadcrumbs are thoroughly saturated and the mixture resembles oatmeal.

Pour the mixture into the slow cooker and cook on high for 4 to 5 hours, until a tester comes out clean. Tilt the lid to vent the slow cooker for the last 30 minutes of the cooking time.

Serve warm.

Hot Apple Cider

Nothing warms you up like a hot cup of apple cider. And nothing smells more like Christmas than warm apples and cinnamon.

YIELD: 15 to 17 servings
PREP TIME: 5 minutes
COOK TIME: 3 hours

INGREDIENTS

2 quarts apple cider

¼ cup orange juice concentrate

¼ cup firmly packed light brown sugar

½ teaspoon ground allspice

2 teaspoons whole cloves

2 cinnamon sticks, to serve

bourbon whiskey, to serve (optional)

Throw everything except the cinnamon sticks into the slow cooker. Cover and simmer on low for 3 hours, stirring occasionally and enjoying the aroma that fills the house. Strain the cider to serve hot with a whole cinnamon stick in each cup. Add bourbon, if using.

Maple Carrots

Tender and sweet and absolutely delicious, these carrots make a wonderful holiday side dish.

YIELD: 6 to 8 servings
PREP TIME: 5 minutes
COOK TIME: 6 hours

INGREDIENTS

4 cups chopped carrots
2 tablespoons honey
½ cup orange juice
1 tablespoon butter
¼ teaspoon ground ginger
½ teaspoon ground cinnamon
¼ teaspoon kosher salt
¼ teaspoon black pepper

Stir all the ingredients together in the slow cooker. Cover and cook on low for 6 hours.

Hanukkah

For those of us confused about how to spell Hanukkah, we get a break. Since the sound of the Hebrew letters can't be directly translated, the many accepted English spellings are all considered correct.

Slow Cooker Kugel

A spin on a classic kugel recipe.

YIELD: 8 to 10 servings
PREP TIME: 20 minutes
COOK TIME: About 2 hours

INGREDIENTS

12 ounces uncooked egg noodles

½ cup dried currants

1 (10.75-ounce) can condensed Cheddar cheese soup

1 cup cottage cheese

¾ cup granulated sugar

2 eggs

1 teaspoon grated orange zest

Spray the slow cooker with cooking spray. Cook the noodles as directed on the package, but stop before they're completely soft. Drain and transfer to the slow cooker. Sprinkle the currants over the noodles.

In a bowl, mix together the soup, cottage cheese, sugar, eggs, and orange zest with a fork. Pour the mixture over the noodles and stir to make sure the noodles are thoroughly coated. Cover and cook on low for 2 hours.

Serve warm.

Old-Fashioned Beef Brisket

It doesn't get more tender, tasty, and comforting than this. Make sure you buy beef brisket, not corned beef or another cut.

YIELD: 16 servings
PREP TIME: 15 minutes
COOK TIME: 8 to 10 hours

INGREDIENTS

2 medium onions, thinly sliced

4 pounds beef brisket

4 garlic cloves, minced

1 tablespoon red wine vinegar

1 tablespoon light brown sugar

2 tablespoons ketchup

⅓ cup water

2 tablespoons all-purpose flour

½ teaspoon kosher salt

⅛ teaspoon black pepper

Place the sliced onions in the slow cooker and top with the brisket, fat-side up. Cover the meat with the garlic. Mix the vinegar, brown sugar, and ketchup in a small bowl and then rub the mixture onto the beef. Pour in the water—at the side of the slow cooker so the glaze doesn't rinse off—to coat the bottom. Cover and cook on low for 8 to 10 hours.

Take the meat out of the slow cooker and set it on a serving plate. Cover tightly with foil to keep it warm.

To make gravy, turn the slow cooker to high. In a small bowl, mix the flour with just enough water to make a smooth mixture and season with the salt and pepper. Whisk the flour mixture into the drippings in the slow cooker and bring to a boil, whisking vigorously until smooth and thickened.

Slice the beef and pass the gravy to ladle over it.

Braised Lamb Shanks

A twist on a classic leg of lamb, these lamb shanks come out tender and juicy, with a wonderful sauce.

YIELD: 4 servings
PREP TIME: 20 minutes
COOK TIME: About 6 hours

INGREDIENTS

1 medium yellow onion, diced

1 cup peeled, diced tomatoes

2 carrots, peeled and diced

2 celery stalks, diced

3 garlic cloves, crushed

2 cups low-sodium chicken stock (homemade is best, if you have it)

1 teaspoon chopped fresh thyme

1 bay leaf

2 tablespoons olive oil

4 lamb shanks, with fat trimmed (about 4 pounds)

1 teaspoon kosher salt, divided

1 teaspoon freshly ground black pepper, divided

1 cup dry red wine

2 tablespoons tomato paste

Spray the inside of the slow cooker with cooking spray. Place the onion, tomatoes, carrots, celery, garlic, chicken stock, thyme, and bay leaf in the slow cooker. Mix together.

Season the lamb shanks with some of the salt and pepper. Heat the olive oil in a large skillet over medium heat and brown the shanks in the hot oil, turning to brown on all sides. Transfer the shanks to the slow cooker.

Pour the red wine into the same skillet, off of from the heat. Return to the stovetop over medium-high heat and simmer, scraping the pan to get all the brown bits. Stir in the tomato paste. Add to the slow cooker, cover, and cook on high for 6 hours.

Remove the lamb shanks from the slow cooker and set aside on a serving dish, and cover to keep warm. Take the bay leaf out of the sauce. Use an immersion blender or a whisk to make the sauce silky smooth. Pass the sauce to serve with the shanks.

Chunky Applesauce

Wonderful for serving on latkes, applesauce is always a welcome part of a Hanukkah feast.

YIELD: 15 to 17 servings
PREP TIME: 5 minutes
COOK TIME: 10 hours

INGREDIENTS

10 Granny Smith apples, peeled, cored, and chunked

½ cup water

1 teaspoon ground cinnamon

1 cup granulated sugar

Stir together all the ingredients in the slow cooker. Cover and cook on low for 10 hours.

Challah Pudding

Here's a terrific way to use leftover challah bread. Try buying day-old stale bread from the store.

YIELD: 6 servings
PREP TIME: 15 minutes
COOK TIME: 4 to 5 hours

INGREDIENTS

5 cups cubed stale challah bread

3 eggs

2 (12-ounce) cans evaporated milk

1 teaspoon vanilla extract

½ cup granulated sugar

1 teaspoon ground cinnamon

¼ teaspoon ground nutmeg

pinch of kosher salt

Spray the slow cooker with cooking spray. Place the cubes of bread in the slow cooker.

Whisk the eggs in a bowl and then mix in all the remaining ingredients. Pour the mixture over the bread cubes, cover, and cook on low for 4 to 5 hours.

Serve warm.

CONVERSIONS

MEASURE	EQUIVALENT	METRIC
1 teaspoon	—	5.0 milliliters
1 tablespoon	3 teaspoons	14.8 milliliters
1 cup	16 tablespoons	236.8 milliliters
1 pint	2 cups	473.6 milliliters
1 quart	4 cups	947.2 milliliters
1 liter	4 cups + 3½ tablespoons	1000 milliliters
1 ounce (dry)	2 tablespoons	28.35 grams
1 pound	16 ounces	453.49 grams
2.21 pounds	35.3 ounces	1 kilogram
325°F/350°F/375°F		165°C/177°C/190°C

PHOTO CREDITS

page 3: Mardi Gras beads © Svetlana Larina/shutterstock.com; party hat © Fotoksa/shutterstock.com; Easter eggs © Kati Molin/shutterstock.com; half dollar © Anusorn P nachol/shutterstock.com; shamrocks © Victor Soares/shutterstock.com; chocolate hearts © Madlen/shutterstock.com

pages 4–10: party hat © Fotoksa/shutterstock.com

page 6: meatballs © judiswinksphotography.com

page 9: cork © Bragin Alexey

pages 11–14: half dollar © Anusorn P nachol/shutterstock.com

pages 15–17: Mardi Gras beads © Svetlana Larina/shutterstock.com

pages 18–24: chocolate hearts © Madlen/shutterstock.com

page 23: chocolate strawberries © judiswinksphotography.com

pages 25–29: shamrocks © Victor Soares/shutterstock.com

page 28: corned beef © judiswinksphotography.com

pages 30–36: Easter eggs © Kati Molin/shutterstock.com

page 32: rabbits © Dmitry Kalinovsky/shutterstock.com

page 35: honey-glazed ham © judiswinksphotography.com

page 37: tulips © esbobeldijk/shutterstock.com; flag © Morgan Lane Photography/shutterstock.com; blocks © JeniFoto/shutterstock.com; maracas © Cindy Shebley/shutterstock.com; Eiffel Tower © Filip Fuxa/shutterstock.com

pages 38–44: maracas © Cindy Shebley/shutterstock.com

page 40: carnitas © judiswinksphotography.com

pages 45–47: tulips © esbobeldijk/shutterstock.com

page 47: peonies © Africa Studio/shutterstock.com

pages 48–50: blocks © JeniFoto/shutterstock.com

pages 51–57: flag © Morgan Lane Photography/shutterstock.com

page 52: pail © Cheryl Ann Quigley/shutterstock.com

page 55: pulled pork © judiswinksphotogrpahy.com

page 57: flag bunting © Johann Helgason/shutterstock.com

pages 58–62: Eiffel Tower © Filip Fuxa/shutterstock.com

page 63: jack-o'-lantern © Loskutnikov/shutterstock.com; beer © HLPhoto/shutterstock.com; cornucopia © JeniFoto/shutterstock.com

pages 64–65: beer © HLPhoto/shutterstock.com

pages 66–70: jack-o'-lantern © Loskutnikov/shutterstock.com

page 68: pork stew © judiswinksphotography.com

pages 71–85: cornucopia © JeniFoto/shutterstock.com

page 73: turkey dinner © judiswinksphotography.com

page 74: dried corn © Madlen

page 78: corn ears © Diana Taliun/shutterstock.com

page 80: Thanksgiving sides © judiswinksphotography.com

page 83: squash © Hintau Aliaksei/shutterstock.com

page 87: gifts boxes © Fotoline/shutterstock.com; dreidels © Noam Armonn/shutterstock.com

pages 88–98: gifts boxes © Fotoline/shutterstock.com

page 93: lamb roast © judiswinksphotography.com

page 94: holly © Vladimir Wrangel/shutterstock.com

page 97: tree © Anteromite/shutterstock.com

pages 99–104: dreidels © Noam Armonn/shutterstock.com

page 100: menorah © Pilar Echevarria/shutterstock.com

page 103: apple © Maks Narodenko/shutterstock.com

page 104: gelt © CLM/shutterstock.com

ABOUT THE AUTHOR

Jonnie Downing comes from a large family, where holiday dinners were real events. Year after year she would watch as her mother slaved away in the kitchen only to be completely exhausted by the time the meal was on the table. After a few years of doing that same thing, Jonnie decided that some of the heavy lifting could happen in the slow cooker.

Now she and her daughter, Elizabeth, run the website CrockpotNinja.com and have a great time finding and creating new recipes for the slow cooker.

ACKNOWLEDGMENTS

Thanks to family and friends for volunteering to be guinea pigs for some of the recipes that didn't make it into this book.